DATE DUE

NOV 1 4 2013			

Demco, Inc. 38-293

Smokeless Tobacco

NOT A SAFE ALTERNATIVE

Tobacco: The Deadly Drug

Smokeless Tobacco

Not a Safe Alternative

by
Katie John Sharp

McLean County Unit #5
201-EJHS

Smokeless Tobacco: Not a Safe Alternative

Copyright © 2009 by Mason Crest Publishers. All rights reserved.
No part of this publication may be reproduced or transmitted in
any form or by any means, electronic or mechanical, including
photocopying, recording, taping, or any information storage and
retrieval system, without permission from the publisher.

MASON CREST PUBLISHERS INC.
370 Reed Road
Broomall, Pennsylvania 19008
(866)MCP-BOOK (toll free)
www.masoncrest.com

First Printing

9 8 7 6 5 4 3 2 1

ISBN 978-1-4222-0241-8
ISBN 978-1-4222-0230-2 (series)
        Library of Congress Cataloging-in-Publication Data
Sharp, Katie John.
Smokeless tobacco : not a safe alternative / Katie John Sharp.
    p. cm. — (Tobacco: the deadly drug)
  Includes bibliographical references and index.
  ISBN 978-1-4222-0241-8   ISBN 978-1-4222-1332-2
  1. Smokeless tobacco—Juvenile literature. I. Title.
  RA1242.T6S42 2009
  613.85—dc22
                            2008023753

Design by MK Bassett-Harvey.
Produced by Harding House Publishing Service, Inc.
www.hardinghousepages.com
Cover design by Peter Culotta.
Printed in The United States of America.

Contents

Introduction

Tobacco has been around for centuries. In fact, it played a major role in the early history of the United States. Tobacco use has fallen into and out of popularity, sometimes based on gender roles or class, or more recently, because of its effects on health. The books in the Mason Crest series Tobacco: The Deadly Drug, provide readers with a look at many aspects of tobacco use. Most important, the series takes a serious look at why smoking is such a hard habit to break, even with all of the available information about its harmful effects.

The primary ingredient in tobacco products that keeps people coming back for another cigarette is nicotine. Nicotine is a naturally occurring chemical in the tobacco plant. As plants evolved over millions of years, they developed the ability to produce chemical defenses against being eaten by animals. Nicotine is the tobacco plant's chemical defense weapon. Just as too much nicotine can make a person feel dizzy and nauseated, so the same thing happens to animals that might otherwise eat unlimited quantities of the tobacco plant.

Nicotine, in small doses, produces mildly pleasurable (rewarding) experiences, leading many people to dose themselves repeatedly throughout the day. People carefully dose themselves with nicotine to maximize the rewarding experience. These periodic hits of tobacco also help people avoid unpleasant (toxic) effects, such as dizziness, nausea, trembling, and sweating, which can occur when someone takes in an excessive amount of nicotine. These unpleasant effects are sometimes seen when a person smokes for the first time.

Although nicotine is the rewarding component of cigarettes, it is not the cause of many diseases that trouble smokers, such as lung cancer, heart attacks, and strokes. Many of the thousands of other chemicals in the cigarette are responsible for the increased risk for these diseases among smokers. In some cases, medical research has identified cancer-causing chemicals in the burning cigarette. More research is needed, because our understanding of exactly how cigarette smoking causes many forms of cancer, lung diseases (emphysema, bronchitis), heart attacks, and strokes is limited, as is our knowledge on the effects of secondhand smoke.

The problem with smoking also involves addiction. But what is addiction? Addiction refers to a pattern of behavior, lasting months to years, in which a person engages in the intense, daily use of a pleasure-producing (rewarding) activity, such as smoking. This type of use has medically and personally negative effects for the person. As an example of negative medical consequences, consider that heavy smoking (nicotine addiction) leads to heart attacks and lung cancer. As an example of negative personal consequences, consider that heavy smoking may cause a loss of friendship, because the friend can't tolerate the smoke and/or the odor.

Nicotine addiction includes tolerance and withdrawal. New smokers typically start with fewer than five cigarettes per day. Gradually, as the body becomes adapted to the presence of nicotine, greater amounts are required to obtain the same rewarding effects, and the person eventually smokes fifteen to twenty or more cigarettes per day. This is tolerance, meaning that more drug is needed to achieve the same rewarding effects. The brain becomes "wired" differently after long-term exposure to nicotine, allowing the brain to tolerate levels of nicotine that would otherwise be toxic and cause nausea, vomiting, dizziness and anxiety.

When a heavy smoker abruptly stops smoking, irritability, headache, sleeplessness, anxiety, and difficulty concentrating all develop within half a day and trouble the smoker for one to two weeks. These withdrawal effects are generally the opposite of those produced by the drug. They are another external sign that the brain has become wired differently because of long-term exposure to nicotine. The withdrawal effects described above are accompanied by craving. For the nicotine addict, craving is a state of mind in which having a cigarette seems the most important thing in life at the moment. For the nicotine addict, craving is a powerful urge to smoke.

Nicotine addiction, then, can be understood as heavy, daily use over months to years (with tolerance and withdrawal), despite negative consequences. Now that we have definitions of *nicotine* and *addiction*, why read the books in this series? The answer is simple: tobacco is available everywhere to persons of all ages. The books in the series TOBACCO: THE DEADLY DRUG are about understanding the beginnings, natural history, and consequences of nicotine addiction. If a teenager smokes at least one cigarette daily for a month, that person has an 80 percent chance of becoming a lifetime, nicotine-addicted, daily smoker, with all the negative consequences.

But the series is not limited to those topics. What are the characteristic beginnings of nicotine addiction? Nicotine addiction typically begins between the ages of twelve and twenty, when most young people decide to try a first cigarette. Because cigarettes are available everywhere in our society, with little restriction on purchase, nearly everyone is faced with the decision to take a puff from that first cigarette. Whether this first puff leads to a lifetime of nicotine addiction depends on several factors. Perhaps the most important factor is DNA (genetics), as twin studies tell us that most of the risk for nicotine addiction is genetic, but there is a large role for nongenetic factors (environment), such as the smoking habits of friends. Research is needed to identify the specific genetic and environmental factors that shape a person's decision to continue to smoke after that first cigarette. Books in the series also address how peer pressure and biology affect one's likelihood of smoking and possibly becoming addicted.

It is difficult to underestimate the power of nicotine addiction. It causes smokers to continue to smoke despite life-threatening events. When heavy smokers have a heart attack, a life-threatening event often directly related to smoking, they spend a week or more in the hospital where they cannot smoke. So they are discharged after enforced abstinence. Even though they realize that smoking contributed strongly to the heart attack, half of them return to their former smoking habits within three weeks of leaving the hospital. This decision to return to smoking increases the risk of a second heart attack. Nicotine addiction can influence powerfully the choices we make, often prompting us to make choices that put us at risk.

TOBACCO: THE DEADLY DRUG doesn't stop with the whys and the hows of smoking and addiction. The series includes books that provide readers with tools they can use to not take that first cigarette, how they can stand up to negative peer pressure, and know when they are being unfairly influenced by the media. And if they do become smokers, books in the series provide information about how they can stop.

If nicotine addiction can be a powerful negative effect, then giving people information that might help them decide to avoid—or stop—smoking makes sense. That is what TOBACCO: THE DEADLY DRUG is all about.

— *Wade Berrettini MD, PhD*

CHAPTER

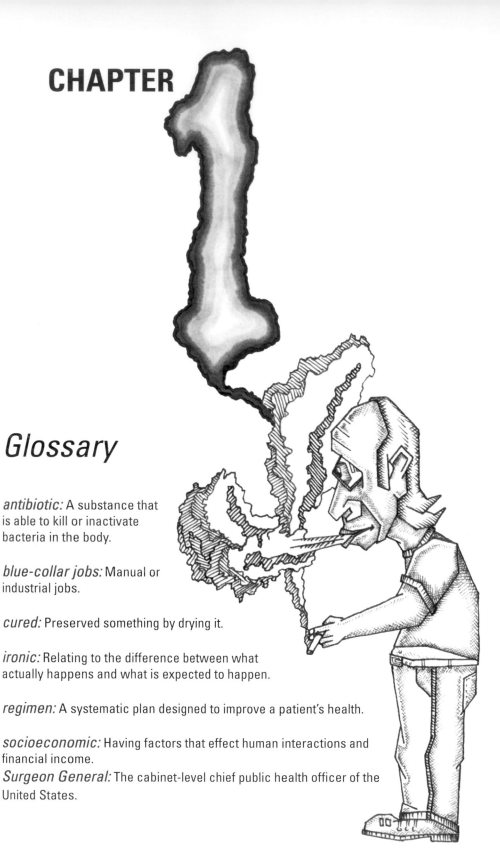

Glossary

antibiotic: A substance that is able to kill or inactivate bacteria in the body.

blue-collar jobs: Manual or industrial jobs.

cured: Preserved something by drying it.

ironic: Relating to the difference between what actually happens and what is expected to happen.

regimen: A systematic plan designed to improve a patient's health.

socioeconomic: Having factors that effect human interactions and financial income.

Surgeon General: The cabinet-level chief public health officer of the United States.

A Closer Look at Smokeless Tobacco

Spit.
Chew.
Chaw.
Dip.
Plug.
Snuff.

All these words have something in common: they are names for smokeless tobacco. Simple, one-syllable names, yes, but they describe a substance whose effects are by no means simple—or harmless—for the human body.

While many people believe placing a "dip of chew" in a cheek or between the lip and gum is better than inhaling smoke from a cigarette, it simply is not true. Any form of tobacco—whether it's smoked, chewed, or snorted—contains chemicals that, over time, can seriously harm the human body.

As the name implies, smokeless tobacco is not inhaled into the lungs. But it is not really "chewed" either, as some of its nicknames might suggest. Instead, it is placed inside the mouth, where it sits for minutes or hours, depending on the user.

A Brief History of Smokeless Tobacco

Native Americans were probably the first people to use smokeless tobacco. After arriving in the Americans in 1492, Christopher Columbus witnessed the native people using leaves of the tobacco plant in several ways. They smoked tobacco in pipes and inhaled it up their noses. They also used it to treat health problems such as toothaches and insect bites and to keep wounds from becoming infected.

When Columbus left North America, he took tobacco plants back to Europe. Soon farmers on both sides of the Atlantic were growing the plant for use as medicine.

The Switch to Cigarettes

When Britain established colonies in North America, the tobacco plant became a popular farming crop. Mass production of tobacco began in 1612, after colonist John Rolfe brought a better variety of tobacco seeds from South America to the Virginia Colony. The plant grew well in the climate along the eastern coast of North America. The colonists shipped most of the tobacco

The TOBACCO – MANUFAC

Engrav'd for the Universal Magazine 1750 for I.Hin

Large tobacco plantations quickly sprang up around colonial America. These required huge amounts of human labor to maintain, so indentured servants and slaves were used.

they cultivated to England—that is, until the American Revolution began in 1775. That's when tobacco growers and manufacturers started to produce tobacco for use among the citizens of what would soon be the United States of America.

Until the late 1800s, most Americans who used tobacco enjoyed smokeless tobacco rather than the smoking variety. In fact, smokeless tobacco was often peddled as a treatment for toothache pain, neuralgia (nerve pain), bleeding gums, and scurvy (a disease caused by a deficiency of vitamin C that affects the teeth, gums, and skin). Smokeless tobacco was even believed to preserve and whiten teeth, and prevent tooth decay. In the late 1800s and early 1900s, however, three things happened that gradually made smoking tobacco more appealing than smokeless tobacco.

First among them was the invention of the cigarette-rolling machine. This new invention allowed cigarette companies to make many cigarettes quickly. The more

Smokeless tobacco has been around for centuries. Spitoons like this were placed in public places so that people would be encouraged not to spit their tobacco on the floor.

cigarettes they could make, the more they could sell—and at cheaper price. Therefore, smoking cigarettes became a less expensive habit than chewing tobacco.

The second thing that increased the popularity of cigarettes began with Louis Pasteur's development of the germ theory of disease. Pasteur claimed microorganisms, or germs, caused disease. We know this to be true today, but at the end of the nineteenth century, people were not easily convinced. For a long time they believed that diseases just happened. When people came to realize that germs cause diseases, and that germs could easily spread from one person to the next, they wanted to take steps to prevent their spread.

Cuspidors and Spittoons

In the 1800s and early 1900s, chewing tobacco was so common that containers called cuspidors and spittoons were available in all kinds of public places into which users could spit out their tobacco-laced saliva. Even the nation's fanciest hotels, including the Plaza in New York and Chicago's Palmer House, provided them. When cigarettes became more popular than smokeless tobacco, however, spittoons and cuspidors slowly faded away. Today these containers made during that era are collectible antiques.

What does the germ theory have to do with chewing tobacco? Well, at the time the theory became popular, scores of people were suffering from tuberculosis (TB), a serious lung disease. Today, when TB occurs, a long *regimen* of *antibiotic* treatment is used to cure it. But in the 1800s, people had no defense against the deadly disease. Once aware of the germ theory, individuals worried that TB could be spread through spit-tobacco juices. This fear steered tobacco users toward the cigarette, which they considered a more sanitary way to get a nicotine fix.

Today, we can appreciate how *ironic* it was that people were so afraid of TB, yet did not realize that smoking cigarettes could also be deadly.

The last thing to turn tobacco users away from chewing tobacco and toward smoking cigarettes was World War I (1914–1918). During that conflict, cigarettes were given freely to American soldiers. This eventually caused the United States to become a nation of smokers.

What's Old Is New Again

At the turn of the twentieth century, the number of people using smokeless tobacco was steadily decreasing. But during the 1970s, it staged a comeback, with an increase of 10 to 11 percent more users each year until 1986. In that year, two things happened to bring the numbers down again—for a little while.

First, a conference on smokeless tobacco was held in Bethesda, Maryland, home of the U.S. National Institutes of Health (NIH). Second, the U.S. *Surgeon General* published his first report on smokeless tobacco. These two events helped create a national awareness of the ill effects smokeless tobacco has on human health. So did the much-publicized case

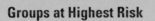

Groups at Highest Risk

American Indians and Alaskan Native people have the highest rates of smokeless-tobacco use. The risks are highest for American Indian and Alaskan Native youth. In a survey of more than two thousand young American Indians between the ages of thirteen and twenty, 21 percent reported some use of smokeless tobacco. And according to a report in a *State of Alaska Epidemiology Bulletin*, high-school-aged Alaskan Native males are twice as likely, and Alaskan Native females are nine times as likely, to use smokeless tobacco as the national rates for other high-school students.

of teenage smokeless-tobacco user Sean Marsee (see chapter 3), the introduction of mandatory warning labels on packages of tobacco, and a ban on certain forms of tobacco advertising. All these factors caused smokeless-tobacco sales to decline. But the drop lasted only about eighteen months; sales and usage of smokeless tobacco bounced back by 1988.

The introduction of warning labels on tobacco packages helped lead to a decrease in the use of smokeless tobacco.

Today, millions of people use smokeless tobacco. According to the U.S. Centers for Disease Control and Prevention (CDC), an estimated 3 percent of adults, 8 percent of high-school students, and 3 percent of middle-schoolers use the stuff. People who use smokeless tobacco choose from two main types: chewing tobacco and snuff. Both are made from the leaves of the tobacco plant, which is grown in twenty-one U.S. states and other areas of the world. In the United States, North Carolina and Kentucky are the largest tobacco producers; they account for about two-thirds of the country's tobacco production. Cigarettes are the main product made from U.S. tobacco; smokeless-tobacco products, in various forms, are next in line.

Chewing Tobacco

Chewing tobacco comes in three forms: twist, plug, and loose leaf. Most of the tobacco leaves used to manufacture chewing tobacco are grown in Wisconsin and Pennsylvania. Though they may come from the same tobacco fields, the three types of chewing tobacco differ in how they are processed and packaged, and in the flavorings added to them. Ingredients such as rum, licorice, sugar, and spices are all used to make chewing tobacco more flavorful.

The process of using chewing tobacco is often referred to as "dipping," "pinching," or "rubbing." When a person uses chewing tobacco, he typically stuffs anywhere from a pinch to as much as a golf ball–sized amount—called a "chaw"—into the cheek. This gives the characteristic swollen-cheeked appearance that is sometimes evident among some professional baseball players (see chapter 4).

Twist

Twist is the oldest form of chewing tobacco. Tobacco companies make this form by twisting or braiding together two or three tobacco leaves while they are still green. The twists are then *cured*, or processed with chemicals. Users cut off a desired amount of a twist and place it between their lip and gum.

Plug

Plug is a small rectangular cake of condensed tobacco. It was the most popular form of chewing tobacco about sixty years ago, but its popularity has declined over the past thirty years.

To make plug, tobacco companies press together cured tobacco leaves in a sugary syrup. Originally, this was done by hand. But since the mid-1800s, the leaves have been pressed between large sheets of tin. The

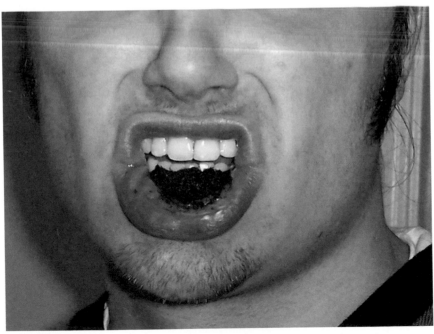

Plugs of tobacco are placed between the lip and gum and kept there.

compressed leaves are then cut into plugs, or flat cakes of tobacco. Users cut a piece off the plug and stick it between the lip and gum.

Loose-Leaf Tobacco

Loose-leaf tobacco is exactly what the name implies. It is made of loose leaves of cured tobacco shredded into small pieces. This form of chewing tobacco was once called "scrap," because it was made from the leftovers—or scrap—of plug-tobacco production. Today, loose-leaf tobacco is by far the most popular form of the three types of chewing tobacco. Often sweetened with different flavors, it is sold loose in bags or in tins.

Like any other kind of tobacco, there are many different brands and types of loose-leaf tobacco.

A person who uses loose-leaf chewing tobacco takes the somewhat sticky stuff and places it into the cheek. Some people cram a lot of tobacco in this small space, while others use only a small pinch.

Spit It Out

After a person places the twist, plug, or loose-leaf tobacco into the mouth, the tobacco just sits there. Within seconds, saliva begins to build up. That's why, every so often, the user has to spit out tobacco-stained saliva—ideally into some kind of container. This need to spit is why chewing tobacco is also called "spit tobacco." Some users do, however, choose to swallow the saliva instead of spitting it out.

The Stuff Called Snuff

Snuff is finely ground or powdered tobacco. It is often packaged loose in small cans called tins, or is available in sachets that look a little like tea bags. There are three types of snuff: dry, moist, and semi-moist. Moist snuff, produced mainly from tobacco leaves grown in Tennessee and Kentucky, is the most popular smokeless tobacco used in the United States.

Snuff users place a pinch, called a "quid," of the stuff between the lower lip and gum. Then, just as with chewing tobacco, they suck on the tobacco and spit out or swallow the saliva that forms.

Some people sniff or inhale loose snuff instead of putting it into the mouth. The appeal of "snorting" snuff is that there

Double Dipping
Some smokeless-tobacco users practice "double dipping." This means they use snuff and chewing tobacco together.

is no saliva to deal with. This allows a person to use smokeless tobacco just about anywhere. As more and more public places become smoke free, this is becom-ing an important feature for smokeless-tobacco users.

Who Chews?

According to the 2005 National Survey on Drug Use and Health, approximately 7.8 million people currently use smokeless tobacco. Though men and boys are much more likely than women and girls to use chewing tobacco or snuff, women and girls do use the stuff. Of the 7.8 million users, just over half a million are female. Just over half a million of all users are children and young adults between the ages of twelve and seventeen.

Another study found that among high-school seniors who chew tobacco, almost 75 percent began by the ninth grade. The U.S. CDC reports that nearly 8 percent of high-school students are current smokeless-tobacco users. The habit is more common among high-school males than females, and Caucasian students are more likely than Hispanic or African American students to use chewing tobacco. Middle-school students use it too. In one survey, about 3 percent of middle-school students said they had used smokeless tobacco at least once in the month before they were asked about it.

Naturally, health experts worry about so many young people using smokeless tobacco. They are also concerned that more and more people of all ages may pick up the habit as the number of states banning indoor smoking grows. Today, Arkansas, Colorado, Washington D.C., Hawaii, New Jersey, and Utah ban smoking in all public places. Other states are sure to follow.

Men are more likely to use chewing tobacco than women, but almost half a million women use smokeless tobacco as well.

And even with all the warnings about the health effects of smokeless tobacco, people—especially younger males—are not slowing down their use of this form of tobacco. Over the past twenty years, smokeless-tobacco use has tripled. Since 1970, it has gone from a product popular mainly among older men to one that is highly sought-after by young men and boys. In 1970, for example, males sixty-five and older were almost six times more likely than eighteen- to twenty-four-year-old males

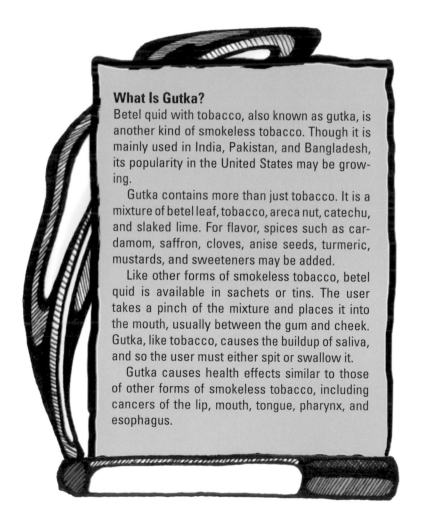

What Is Gutka?

Betel quid with tobacco, also known as gutka, is another kind of smokeless tobacco. Though it is mainly used in India, Pakistan, and Bangladesh, its popularity in the United States may be growing.

Gutka contains more than just tobacco. It is a mixture of betel leaf, tobacco, areca nut, catechu, and slaked lime. For flavor, spices such as cardamom, saffron, cloves, anise seeds, turmeric, mustards, and sweeteners may be added.

Like other forms of smokeless tobacco, betel quid is available in sachets or tins. The user takes a pinch of the mixture and places it into the mouth, usually between the gum and cheek. Gutka, like tobacco, causes the buildup of saliva, and so the user must either spit or swallow it.

Gutka causes health effects similar to those of other forms of smokeless tobacco, including cancers of the lip, mouth, tongue, pharynx, and esophagus.

to engage in the smokeless-tobacco habit. By 1991, however, younger males were 50 percent more likely than older men to be users. The switch from the older generation to the younger one is especially prevalent for use of moist snuff. From 1970 to 1991, the regular use of this form of snuff by males between the ages seventeen and twenty-four grew nearly ten times.

Despite the bad news about young adults and smokeless tobacco, there *is* good news: smokeless-tobacco use in general is decreasing. Still, many men, women, boys, and girls continue to use smokeless tobacco. In some states, the problem is severe. In Kentucky, for example, nearly one out of every four high-school-aged boys uses smokeless tobacco. Other states with similar statistics include South Dakota, West Virginia, and Oklahoma.

Who's at Risk for Addiction?

Studies and surveys show that certain people are more likely than others to become regular smokeless-tobacco users. While no one can predict exactly who will start using smokeless tobacco, it is important to create a picture of the typical user. This helps health-care professionals, teachers, parents, and others know whom to target in their efforts to prevent its use in the first place. Research shows the typical smokeless tobacco user:

- is between the ages of eighteen and twenty-five
- is male. (Smokeless tobacco use is fifteen times more common among men than women. Over 6 percent of

men use smokeless tobacco, while only .4 percent
of women use it.)

- lives in a southern or north/central state. (Smokeless-tobacco use is more common in southern
states and in rural areas with low socioeconomic
status than it is in other states or in high-income
areas.)
- plays sports. (Smokeless tobacco is a popular
habit in certain sports, including baseball, hockey,
and the rodeo. At one time, 40 percent of professional baseball players said they were smokeless-
tobacco users.)
- has a full-time job. (Just about 4.5 percent of people
with full-time jobs use smokeless tobacco, while
2.2 percent of part-time workers use it. However,
people who do not have jobs at all come pretty
close to the full-timers, at 4.1 percent. Among
those who are employed,
smokeless-tobacco use is
most prevalent among
people with blue-
collar jobs and
those in service
occupations.)
- smokes. (Smoke-
less-tobacco users
often smoke cigarettes
as well.)

Why would anyone want
to stick tobacco leaves
inside his or her mouth? Curios-
ity, ignorance, and peer pressure are
just some of the reasons a person might

try smokeless tobacco for the first time. But why would anyone continue to engage in a habit that is expensive, dangerous, and considered by many to be disgusting? The answer is nicotine, the highly addictive drug that occurs naturally in the tobacco plant.

CHAPTER

Glossary

hormone: A chemical substance produced in the body that circulates in body fluids and helps control cell activity.

tolerant: No longer responsive to a substance that has been taken over a prolonged period.

Why Chewers Choose to Chew

Nicotine is the main reason anyone uses any form of tobacco, from chewing tobacco and snuff to cigars, pipes, and cigarettes. People use nicotine because it makes them feel good, and it's this feeling that makes them want to chew or dip or smoke over and over again. The feeling comes on quick and strong, but it does not last very long. So in order to get the feeling again, a tobacco user has to repeat her habit—smoke another cigarette or dip another pinch of chew—several times each day.

The Drug Called Nicotine

The tobacco plant consists of more than four thousand different chemicals. Nicotine is just one of them, but it makes up about 5 percent of the plant's weight. Like all drugs, nicotine is a chemical. It is made up of the natural elements carbon, hydrogen, nitrogen, and oxygen bonded together in a very specific way.

As with most addictive substances, humans have developed several ways to get nicotine into their bodies. The drug is able to enter the human body through three different body tissues: the skin, the lungs, and the mucous membranes that line the inside of certain parts of the body including the nose, mouth, throat, esophagus, and stomach. Nicotine enters the small blood vessels that line these different body tissues. After entering the bloodstream, the drug travels to the brain. From there, it is delivered to other areas of the body. Both tobacco that is smoked and smokeless tobacco are effective at delivering nicotine to the body—but in different ways.

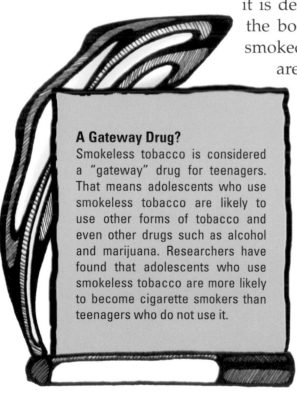

A Gateway Drug?

Smokeless tobacco is considered a "gateway" drug for teenagers. That means adolescents who use smokeless tobacco are likely to use other forms of tobacco and even other drugs such as alcohol and marijuana. Researchers have found that adolescents who use smokeless tobacco are more likely to become cigarette smokers than teenagers who do not use it.

Inhaling Smoke

The most common—and quickest—way to get nicotine into the bloodstream is through inhalation, or by breathing in the smoke of a cigarette. (People who smoke cigars and pipes don't generally inhale the smoke.) Once cigarette

Inhaling the smoke from a cigarette or cigar is one of the most efficient ways of getting nicotine into the bloodstream.

smoke is inhaled into the mouth, it quickly travels to the lungs.

The lungs are lined with millions of alveoli, or tiny air sacs. Nicotine enters the blood vessels that lie just beneath the surface of the alveoli. Because of their shape, alveoli provide lots of surface area from which nicotine can enter the bloodstream. In fact, alveoli have ninety times more surface area than skin. This means a lot more nicotine can enter the bloodstream through alveoli than through skin. Once in the bloodstream, nicotine travels to the brain. There it sets off a series of reactions that cause several different effects on the body.

"Chewing" Tobacco

Nicotine can also enter the bloodstream through the mucous membranes that line the gums and cheeks. When a person places a pinch or wad of tobacco leaves inside the mouth, nicotine from the tobacco travels within seconds through the mucous membranes that line the gums and cheeks. The nicotine quickly enters the blood vessels just beneath the surface of the mucous membranes and flows into the bloodstream. From there, it travels to the brain, just as it does when inhaled.

How Nicotine Affects the Body

Nicotine changes how the brain—and the body—function. It is a strange drug because it can both energize and relax a person, depending on how much a person uses and how often the individual uses it. These different effects depend on what happens inside the brain when it's under the influence of nicotine.

Nicotine and Neurotransmitters

The brain is made up of cells called neurons, or nerve cells. Nerve cells communicate with each other by releasing chemical messengers called neurotransmitters. Each neurotransmitter is like a key that fits only one lock on the surface of the brain cells. These "locks" are called receptors. When a neurotransmitter locks into its specific receptor, it causes the nerve cell to send a particular message to a part of the body.

Nicotine has the same chemical makeup as a neurotransmitter called acetylcholine. Acetylcholine plays a role in many body functions, including the movement of muscles, breathing, heart rate, learning, and memory. It also causes the release of other neurotransmitters that affect such things as mood and appetite.

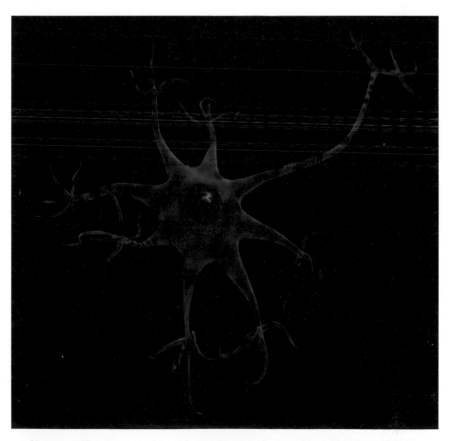

Neurons, like the one shown here, communicate with each other through neurotransmitters. Nicotine replaces one of these chemicals, called acetylcholine.

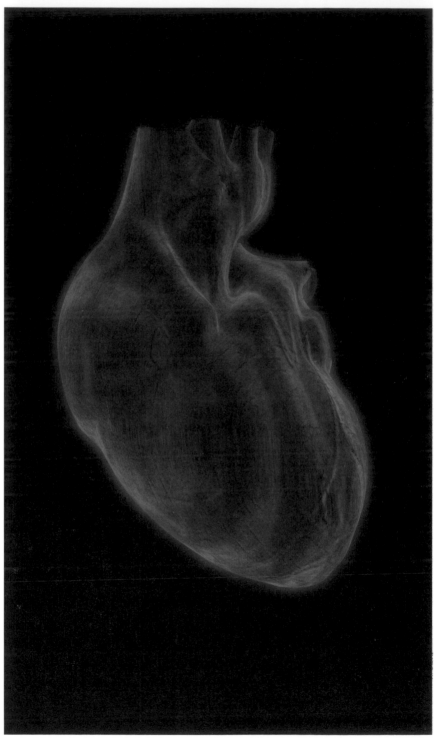

Nicotine causes the release of adrenaline, which, among other things, can increase a person's heartbeat and blood pressure.

Because acetylcholine and nicotine have a similar structure, nicotine can mimic acetylcholine. That means nicotine can lock onto the acetylcholine receptors on nerve cells and then cause those nerve cells to react in the same way acetylcholine would. However, the reactions that nicotine causes are not always identical to those caused by acetylcholine. For example, when acetylcholine locks onto its receptor, the heart starts beating faster. Nicotine also causes an increase in heart rate, but it may make the heart beat even faster than acetylcholine would.

Nicotine also affects the neurotransmitter dopamine. Dopamine plays a role in emotions and in feelings of pleasure and pain. When a person smokes a cigarette or uses smokeless tobacco, nicotine causes a release of dopamine. This, in turn, brings on feelings of pleasure, but these feelings don't last very long. That's one reason a person who uses tobacco may smoke or dip several times each day: he wants to get that good feeling back.

Nicotine and Hormones

Nicotine also causes release of the *hormone* adrenaline. This hormone is often called the "fight-or-flight" hormone. It gets this name from the fact that it is designed to help us when we are in danger. As soon as the brain perceives danger, it releases adrenaline. The hormone immediately gives our muscles the energy they need to either fight the danger or run away from it.

Whenever you are startled by something, you will probably feel the effects of adrenaline. They include rapid heartbeat, increased blood pressure, and rapid shallow breathing. Because nicotine causes a release of adrenaline, these are the immediate side effects of using tobacco.

Nicotine may also block the body's ability to absorb insulin, another hormone. Insulin tells the body's cells to take up excess glucose, or sugar, from the blood. For example, when you eat a candy bar, the brain senses the increase in blood sugar and releases insulin. The insulin then instructs the cells to absorb the glucose in an effort to restore balance to the bloodstream.

Because nicotine blocks this reaction, the drug causes smokers and chewers to become somewhat hyperglycemic; in other words, they have more sugar than normal in the blood. Some people think nicotine curbs the appetite, because often people eat less when they smoke or chew tobacco. This nicotine-induced hyperglycemia could be one reason why. The body and brain may sense the excess sugar in the blood caused by blocked insulin, and then send a message to the brain that the body is not hungry.

Nicotine from Cigarettes vs. Smokeless Tobacco

Cigarette smoke contains 8 to 20 milligrams of nicotine, depending on the brand. Between 1 and 2 milligrams are absorbed into the body when a person smokes. Smokeless tobacco packs a more intense nicotine punch, but it is hard to say just how many milligrams of nicotine a smokeless-tobacco user exposes herself to each time she dips. A new user might dip just a small pinch, while a person with a twenty-five–year habit might go for a golf ball–sized amount each time he uses. This much is known: the nicotine content of a whole can of dip or snuff is about 144 milligrams.

According to the National Cancer Institute, the average amount of nicotine absorbed from smokeless tobacco is three to four times that absorbed from a cigarette. Chewing tobacco delivers about 4.5 milligrams of nicotine per "chaw," while snuff delivers about 3.6 milligrams per "pinch." So a person who uses eight to ten dips or chews a day gets the same amount of nicotine as a smoker who smokes thirty to forty cigarettes in that same time period.

The Road to Addiction

Nicotine's effects last only about forty minutes to two hours. Because tobacco users enjoy those effects—the feelings of pleasure, the lack of appetite, and so on—they want to continue to experience them. The only way to do that, however, is to have another cigarette or take another dip of chew. What's more, the body becomes *tolerant* to nicotine's effects, so it needs more and more nicotine to get the same effects. All this is why it is so easy for people to quickly move from enjoying a small pinch of smokeless tobacco a couple times a day to craving a much larger amount more often each day.

Once a person starts using smokeless tobacco, nicotine makes it difficult to quit because the drug is extremely addictive. A person is addicted to a drug when she cannot

Faster at Cancer, Too?
According to a recent medical study, smokeless tobacco is not only more efficient than cigarettes at delivering nicotine to the body, it may also be more effective at delivering cancer-causing substances.

Researchers compared 182 snuff users with 420 cigarette smokers and found that snuff users were exposed to higher amounts of nitrosamines—chemicals known to cause lung and other cancers in animals—than the cigarette smokers. While some tobacco companies suggest that smokeless tobacco products are a safe alternative to cigarettes, this study demonstrates that is simply not true.

control the need for that drug—even when she knows it can cause serious health consequences, including death.

In the Beginning

Imagine a young boy who is curious about smokeless tobacco. Maybe he has watched someone on television, at a sporting event, or even at home with a lump in his cheek and spitting every now and then. *What is that stuff?* he may ask himself. *What does it taste like? How does it feel to use it?*

Or maybe the boy tries smokeless tobacco because his peers lay on the pressure and convince him it's harmless. "One time won't kill you," they say. "Are you afraid?" "Are you chicken?"

Perhaps the boy wants to prove to himself and others that he is no longer a little kid. He thinks, *Kids don't use chewing tobacco, right? Only adults do.*

For whatever reason, the boy decides to get a pouch of loose-leaf chewing tobacco. Then he hides in his room, takes a pinch of the sticky substance, and places it into his mouth.

Nicotine Takes Hold

If the boy is not completely turned off by the taste or the instant feelings of dizziness or nausea, he keeps the tobacco in place and soon begins to spit out brown-stained saliva. After about thirty minutes, the tobacco loses its licorice flavor and the effects of the nicotine wear off. Is that the end of it? Will the boy ever put tobacco inside his mouth again?

Chances are he will. After a couple days or so, he'll use the last bit from the pouch. And he'll more than likely figure out a way to get another pouch—and then another. The boy will continue using smokeless tobacco

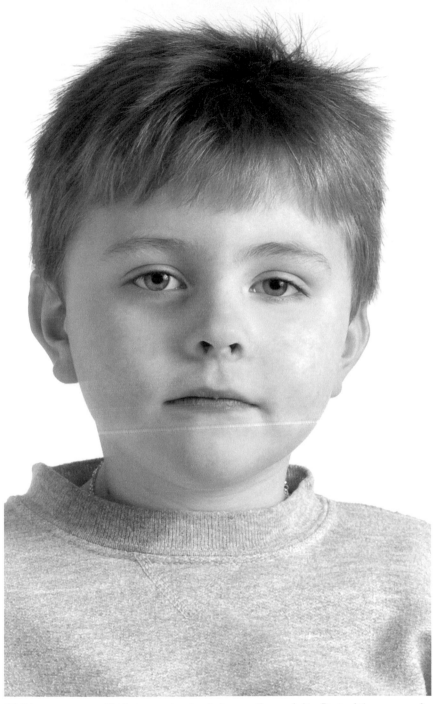

Children are more likely to start using tobacco than adults. Part of the reason for this is their susceptibility to peer pressure.

Historic Thoughts on Nicotine

Hygiene for Young People, a textbook for students in "advanced reader grade[s]," copyright 1884 and 1885, had this to say about nicotine:

> Tobacco, a powerful narcotic, contains a substance called nicotine. A single drop, if put on the tongue of a dog, will soon kill the animal. An ordinary cigar contains nicotine enough to kill two men, if taken pure.
>
> One has to learn to like tobacco. Boys who try it, know that at first it gives them headache, dizziness, and sickness at the stomach. Their poor bodies try to tell them they are taking a poison.
>
> If they keep on, the nicotine deadens their nerves, so they do not feel these effects, though they are more or less injured all the time.

The book went on to say:

> A boy who uses tobacco runs the risk of being dwarfed in body, mind, and soul; of becoming a nervous, sickly man, with a weak memory and a feeble heart.
>
> Physicians agree that many and serious troubles result from its use, even by adults; it is certain that growing boys can never indulge in it with safety.
>
> An eminent physician Dean of one of the leading medical colleges in this country (Dr. A. B. Palmer, of the University of Michigan), says that young men who learn to smoke or chew tobacco, destroy on an average, by so doing, much of the enjoyment and value, and at least one-tenth of the length of their lives.
>
> As with other narcotics, using a little makes one long for more; the boy who begins with one or two cigars a day, soon increases the number.
>
> Many men who are now slaves to this poison, would gladly be free from it; and very few tobacco-users would advise their sons to adopt the expensive, uncleanly, and worse than useless habit.

Today it is known that nicotine is not a narcotic. The term "narcotic" is an older term (no longer preferred) that refers to drugs such as morphine used to treat severe pain.

because he enjoys the feeling he gets from it, and he'll probably think he can quit anytime.

The truth is, he won't be able to stop. In almost no time at all, nicotine takes hold of the brain. And then, not only will he enjoy the feeling brought on by tobacco, he won't be able to stand being without it. If he does try to quit, he'll probably have a difficult time doing so. Chances are, he will fail.

The Symptoms of Addiction

Most people who try smokeless tobacco can become addicted. Once a person is addicted to nicotine, it is hard to quit chewing or smoking. In fact, when people who are addicted to nicotine try to give up the habit, they almost immediately experience withdrawal symptoms. These symptoms usually include intense cravings for nicotine, increased appetite, irritability, sleep problems, nervousness, and depression. When a person can't quit, she is likely to suffer the adverse health effects of the habit. Unfortunately, using smokeless tobacco has other health consequences as well.

CHAPTER 3

Glossary

CAT scan: A diagnostic test in which cross-sectional images of a part of the body are formed through computerized axial tomography and displayed on a computer screen.
cholesterol: A steroid alcohol found in animal tissue, bile, blood, and eggs that has been linked to heart disease.

cholesterol: A steroid alcohol found in animal tissue, bile, blood, and eggs that has been linked to heart disease.

(COPD): A lung disease generally characterized by irreversible airway obstruction.

emphysema: A chronic lung disease in which the air sacs are dilated and lack flexibility, leading to breathing difficulties.

larynx: The box-shaped cartilage part of the respiratory tract between the root of the tongue and the trachea; also called the voice box.

lymph nodes: Oval bodies located in the lymphatic system that produce and store cells that filter out microorganisms.

pharynx: The throat.

Chew on This: The Health Effects of Smokeless Tobacco

Unfortunately, many people believe that chewing tobacco is a safe alternative to smoking cigarettes. They think the only real problem with smoking is that it causes lung cancer. Smokeless tobacco is just that—smokeless—they reason, so the lungs are safe from harm. No lung cancer, no problem—right?

Wrong.

Lung cancer is not the only health problem associated with smoking cigarettes. People who choose to smoke are at risk for a long list of serious health problems, and that's not just because a smoker inhales the smoke into the lungs. It's because tobacco contains thousands of chemicals that can wreak havoc inside the human body, no matter how they get there.

Because various tobacco products are used differently, each causes its own set of health problems. Some of these problems are similar among tobacco products; others are more prevalent among users of a certain form of tobacco.

The Health Effects of Smoking

Smoking is not good for a person's health, regardless of his or her age, but the longer a person smokes, the greater the health risks.

Children and teenagers who pick up the habit put themselves at increased risk for a range of health problems that include:

- coughing
- shortness of breath
- production of excess phlegm or mucus
- respiratory illnesses such as colds and bronchitis
- reduced physical fitness
- poor lung growth and function
- worse overall health
- addiction to nicotine

A teenager who is addicted to nicotine is at an increased risk of continuing to smoke into adulthood. In fact, research shows almost 90 percent of adult smokers started at or before age nineteen. People who begin smoking in their teens have a harder time kicking the habit than do individuals who begin in their twenties or later. What's more, teenagers who continue to smoke typically increase the number of cigarettes they use each day. That's because, over time, their bodies build up a

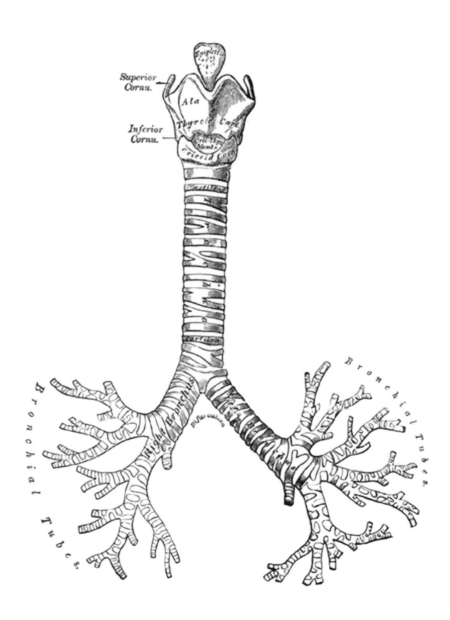

Smoking causes lung problems, including coughing and other signs of poor lung function.

tolerance to the effects of nicotine. And the longer a person smokes, and the more cigarettes he smokes, the more likely he is to develop worsening health problems.

In addition to the other health problems already listed, an adult who uses cigarettes long term may experience:

- cancer of the lungs, bladder, mouth, *pharynx, larynx,* esophagus, cervix, kidney, stomach, and blood
- heart disease, including high blood pressure and stroke
- lung diseases such as *chronic obstructive pulmonary disease (COPD)* and *emphysema*
- problems of the female reproductive system that can affect the health of both the woman/mother and her children
- weakened bones

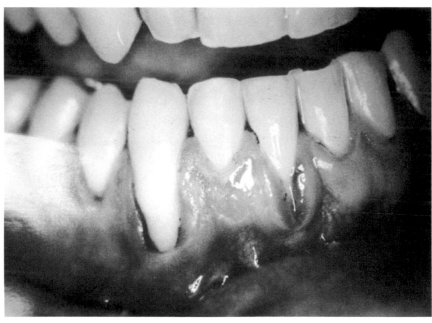

Smokeless tobacco can cause various mouth and gum problems, including gingivitis and tooth loss.

Health Effects of Smokeless Tobacco

While the risks for developing heart disease and cancer from smoking are greater than from use of smokeless tobacco, smokeless tobacco is by no means harmless. Smokeless tobacco has plenty of adverse side effects, including oral health problems, heart trouble, leukoplakia, and cancer.

Oral Health Problems

Perhaps the most obvious health problems caused by smokeless-tobacco use are those that occur inside the mouth. After all, the tobacco—whether it's chewing tobacco or snuff—just sits inside the mouth.

Fairly immediate and less severe side effects of using smokeless tobacco include brown stains on the teeth, mouth sores, and bad breath. Over time, it can also deaden the taste buds so the smokeless-tobacco user cannot taste food as well as before starting the habit.

Smokeless tobacco often contains a lot of sugar. In fact, sugar makes up one-fifth of the content of some brands of chewing tobacco. We all know what sugar does to teeth: it causes cavities. According to a study by the NIH and the CDC, people who use chewing tobacco are four times more likely than nonusers to have tooth decay, especially on the root surfaces of the teeth. Anyone who has ever needed a root canal knows how serious and expensive this can be.

In addition to the damage caused by sugar, chewing tobacco contains tiny rough pieces of tobacco leaves that can irritate gums and scratch away enamel on teeth. Enamel is a hard, thin, see-through layer made mostly of calcium that protects the teeth. Enamel also serves as the surface for chewing, grinding, and crushing food. Without enamel, teeth are much more vulnerable to cavities and other forms of tooth decay.

Sugar and irritants in smokeless tobacco can also cause gums to recede, or pull away from the teeth, especially in the area of the mouth where the tobacco is held. Over time, this can develop into gum disease— gingivitis— and possibly tooth loss.

Heart Trouble

When nicotine from smokeless tobacco enters the body, it raises the heart rate, increases blood pressure, and con-stricts—or narrows—blood vessels. Some studies show that these factors may put users at increased risk of hav-ing a heart attack or stroke. People who use smokeless tobacco also have higher *cholesterol* levels than those who don't use tobacco, and high cholesterol is another risk factor for heart disease.

Leukoplakia

People who use smokeless tobacco often develop a con-dition of the mouth called leukoplakia. In fact, studies have found that the condition occurs in three out of four regular users of smokeless-tobacco products.

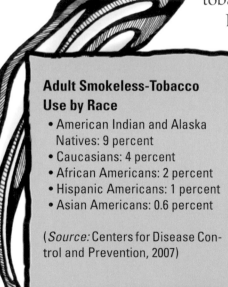

Adult Smokeless-Tobacco Use by Race
• American Indian and Alaska Natives: 9 percent
• Caucasians: 4 percent
• African Americans: 2 percent
• Hispanic Americans: 1 percent
• Asian Americans: 0.6 percent

(*Source:* Centers for Disease Con-trol and Prevention, 2007)

Leukoplakia causes thick, white patches on the mouth's soft tissue,. These patches can appear on the gums, the inside of the cheeks, and the tongue. They cannot be scraped off, and they are often considered precancerous. That means if a person has the condition, it could develop into oral cancer; studies show that between

2 and 6 percent of leukoplakia cases evolve into cancer. Leukoplakia is a very real danger to people who use smokeless tobacco.

Most instances of leukoplakia go away on their own—if the irritant that causes it is removed. In other words, it often goes away if the person quits using smokeless tobacco.

Cancer

According to the CDC, smokeless tobacco contains twenty-eight carcinogens (cancer-causing agents). Because of this, people who use smokeless tobacco are at increased risk for several different cancers. Oral cancer, which includes cancers of the mouth, throat, cheeks, gums, lips, and tongue, is the most common cancer

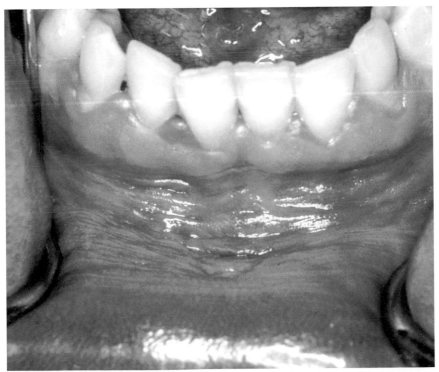

Oral cancers associated with smokeless tobacco affect the mouth, gums, and tongue.

risk among smokeless-tobacco users. When necessary, surgery to remove any of these cancerous areas can leave the jaw, chin, neck, or face disfigured.

Smokeless tobacco is also linked to other forms of cancer. Some of the cancer-causing agents in tobacco can get into the lining of the esophagus, pharynx, larynx, stomach, pancreas, and bladder. This is why smokeless tobacco has been associated with cancers in each of these areas of the body.

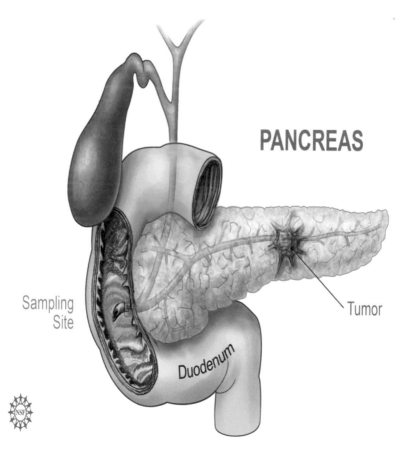

Pancreatic cancer is one of the possible side effects of smokeless tobacco.

Girls Do It Too

While statistics show that most smokeless-tobacco users are boys and men, some girls and women do take up the habit. They have the same risks as male users for suffering the same health consequences.

Jane Imholte was a cigarette smoker and had been for three years when she decided to try chewing tobacco. She was sixteen years old and about to take off on a three-week backpacking trip to Wyoming. A friend also going on the trip told Jane that her smoking might make breathing and hiking difficult at high altitudes. He suggested she try spit tobacco as an alternative to smoking and told her how to use it. In the journal *Tobacco Control*, Jane explained her first experience with chewing tobacco:

> I remember the sickly, minty smell....Nicotine was not new to me, until my first dip. The buzz I got was stronger than one from any other substance I had tried at that point. My head spun, my heart raced, and an incredible surge swept through my body. Nauseous and dizzy, I had to sit down immediately. So this was chew, I thought. I didn't get sick, and it didn't even hurt my mouth. After a few more dips, however, I came to relish the biting sting that was the chew, tearing up my gums.

A Bad Habit Quickly Forms

Jane stocked up on chewing tobacco for her journey. By the time she returned home, she was chewing all day, every day. She liked the idea that she could chew everywhere and anywhere, even in places where she could never smoke such as movie theaters, on the bus to school, in her bedroom at home, and even during classes. She explained how chewing tobacco made her feel and why she continued to use it:

> I felt like a biker, an outlaw, someone with whom not to mess. If I was going to be attractive, it would be on my terms, chew and all. Buying it was never a problem largely because of the surprised clerks: "What's a nice girl like you doing with chew?" Their attitude and that of others was exactly why I continued to chew. I *was* a nice girl, for the most part I managed to stay out of trouble. Chew felt like the equivalent of a tattoo to me. It set me apart. . . . Chew was to me what cigarettes were to women of the 19th century. I had come a long way, baby.

A Role Model?

During college, Jane continued to enjoy being outside and worked as a trail guide for young people. She also continued her chewing habit. Jane says she enjoyed the freedom to spit on the ground or wherever she pleased. Years later, however, Jane admitted to being horrified that, as a trail guide, she had been a leader to young people, including adolescent girls who "too often thought I was the coolest thing they'd ever known."

Jane tried to keep her addiction hidden from those girls, and she thought she was pretty good at it. Those who did find out despite Jane's efforts were often "disgusted and disappointed" in her. Looking back at photographs from those days, Jane says, "I am dismayed to see that most of them show me smiling with a bulging lip. I had thought I was so discreet."

Time to Quit

During her sophomore year at college, Jane visited her

Smokeless-Tobacco Use by Youth

Percentages of High-School-Aged Students Who Reported Current Use of Smokeless Tobacco

- Total: 8 percent
- Males: 13.6 percent
- Females: 2.2 percent
- Breakdown by Race: 10 percent Caucasian, 5.1 percent Hispanic, 1.7 percent African American

Percentages of Middle-School-Aged Students Who Reported Current Use of Smokeless Tobacco

- Total: 3 percent
- Males: 4 percent
- Females: 2 percent
- Breakdown by Race: 3 percent Caucasian, 4 percent Hispanic, 2 percent African American

(*Source:* Centers for Disease Control and Prevention, 2007)

Sean Marsee, a high school football star, became addicted to smokeless tobacco—with tragic consequences.

dentist. Upon looking in her mouth, he immediately noticed that something was not right. Her gums had receded on one side; the damage was slight but could not be reversed. Did that convince her to quit chewing? Not right away. She did quit smoking, but quitting smokeless tobacco proved to be much harder for Jane.

I still got a buzz, and I had come to love the flavor and the security of that little pinch in my mouth. But eventually, chewing no longer emboldened me, it embarrassed me. I was a health conscious, role modeling, college educated woman who didn't look tough, just stupid.

Jane finally kicked the chewing-tobacco habit when she was twenty-three years old. She was moved to action after reading about Bill Tuttle, the major league baseball player who lost his life to oral cancer (see chapter 4). His story gave Jane has given her the inspiration to never chew again.

A Star Athlete

Close your eyes and imagine a person who uses chewing tobacco. What kind of individual do you see? Chances are you don't see a clean-cut, star high-school athlete. You might think such a person would never allow any form of tobacco into his or her body, but in fact, all kinds of people chew tobacco—including athletes. And like anyone else who decides to chew tobacco, star athletes, who have everything going for them, can suffer the health consequences of that decision.

Poor Reasoning

Sean Marsee was a star athlete at his high school in Ada, Oklahoma. He had won an impressive twenty-eight medals at high-school track meets in his young career. Sean was in great physical shape and had always taken great care of his body. He ate healthy foods, lifted weights, and ran five miles a day for six months of the year. Sean didn't smoke cigarettes or drink alcohol. He did, however, use what he thought were "safe" forms of tobacco—chewing tobacco and snuff. He had since he was twelve years old.

Like most people who start chewing tobacco, Sean quickly became addicted to nicotine. At one point, he was polishing off a can of snuff every day and a half. His mother caught on to Sean's addiction not long after he started, but her son paid no attention to her lectures about the dangers of tobacco. He knew plenty of other people—including his teammates—who also chewed, and he told her his coach knew about his habit and didn't seem to think much about it. Sean also listed all the professional athletes he knew of who chewed tobacco. If they were doing it, he reasoned, how could it be all that dangerous?

Oral Lesions Revealed in One Study

Back in the 1980s, 184 American Indian students in grades 7 through 12, who reported regular use of smokeless tobacco were examined for oral lesions. Oral lesions, "defined as any white or red wrinkled area in the mouth or buccal mucosa," were present in 37 percent of these young, smokeless-tobacco users.

Sean would soon find out just how dangerous chewing tobacco could be.

Bad News

One day during his senior year, Sean came home and told his mother that his tongue hurt. She looked inside his mouth and discovered a red sore the size of a half-dollar on his tongue. She took him to a doctor, who ordered tests. When the results came back, the doctor recommended that Sean have part of his tongue removed.

Soon after high-school graduation, Sean had the surgery. The doctor had to remove more of the tongue than he originally thought would be necessary. Sean, they found, had cancer.

The Cancer Spreads

As Sean was getting ready to begin follow-up cancer treatment, doctors discovered a newly swollen lymph node on his neck. This meant the cancer had already spread, and Sean had to have neck surgery. Then his doctor recommended that Sean have his right-side lower jaw removed, as well as the *lymph nodes*, muscles, and blood vessels in that area. Sean agreed to all of it except the jawbone; he did not want his jawbone removed. His doctor performed the surgery on June 20.

By August, Sean was feeling better and upbeat about his prognosis. But just a few months later, in October, he started having headaches. A *CAT scan* showed the cancer had spread once again. Sean was in for more surgery. According to whyquit.com,

Sean endured ten hours of surgery, and when it was over, he had "four huge drains coming from a foot-long crescent wound, a breathing tube sticking out of a hole in his throat, a feeding tube through his nose, and two tubes in his arms."

A Sad Loss

Sean was home for Christmas that year and was even feeling upbeat. But then in January, he found new lumps in his left cheek. The cancer had spread once again, but this time it took his life. Sadly, Sean died in February, at the age of nineteen, just ten months after he had first discovered that red spot on his tongue. Before he died, Sean told his mother that he wished he could visit the high-school locker room to show the athletes what a person who uses chewing tobacco looks like. He knew his appearance would convince young athletes, who are often concerned about their looks, of the need to stop using tobacco.

Sean's mother believes Sean's legacy is having his story spread and, hopefully, "keeping other kids from dying."

It Can Happen to You

It might be easy to read the list of health problems chewing tobacco can cause and then simply toss it aside. Too often, people think such things will never happen to them, so they keep on indulging in their habit. But in fact, the health consequences of using smokeless tobacco are very real for everyone. There are plenty of stories about people who have had to endure the pain and suffering that their addiction so often causes. Smokeless tobacco has an especially long history among many athletes, particularly baseball players.

CHAPTER 4

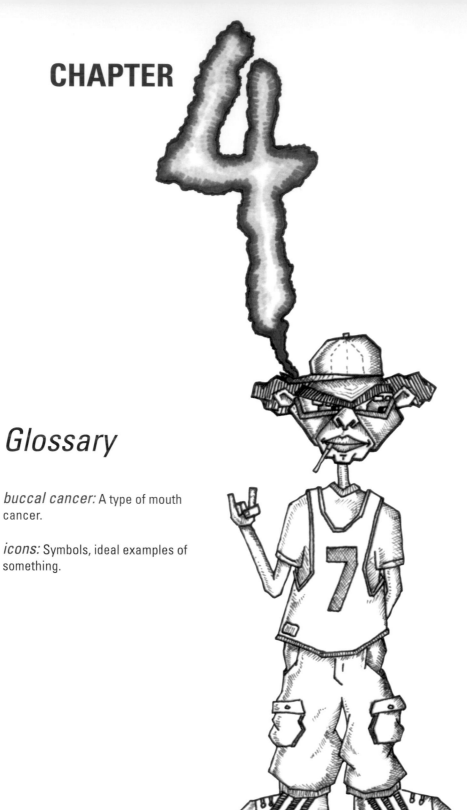

Glossary

buccal cancer: A type of mouth cancer.

icons: Symbols, ideal examples of something.

Smokeless Tobacco and Sports

For years, smokeless tobacco and baseball have gone hand in hand. Since baseball was first played, players have been seen batting, throwing, and fielding while sporting a bulging cheek of tobacco.

And while, yes, major league baseball players are grown men who have the right to choose whether or not they use smokeless tobacco, a large portion of baseball fans are children—who look up to baseball players as *icons*, heroes, and role models. Many young baseball fans are quick to pick up the habits of their heroes. They want to throw and bat like them, and they want to wear their numbers on their backs.

Baseball and smokeless tobacco are often linked in people's minds. This can
lead some young adults to start using chewing tobacco...after all, if their favorite
athlete does it, it can't be too bad for you, can it?

When a young baseball fan sees his favorite player sporting a golf ball–sized bulge in his cheek, he may think that's pretty cool. He might want to use smokeless tobacco too. After all, if his favorite player does it, how bad can it be?

The effects athletes' habits have on young fans is just one reason why there has been a push to convince baseball players and those in other sports to forgo the smokeless-tobacco habit—or least to hide it from their fans. This effort seems to be paying off, as fewer players are indulging in the habit and more are trying to quit.

Not You Too, Babe
Pitcher and outfielder Babe Ruth, a baseball legend who played the game from 1914 to 1935, used smokeless tobacco. He even admitted to swallowing a plug every now and again. Ruth died in 1948, at age fifty-two, of an oropharyngeal tumor, or cancer of the mouth and throat. Most tumors of this kind are caused by tobacco use.

One Player's Story

Bill Tuttle was a great baseball player. From 1952 to 1962, he covered the outfield for the Detroit Tigers, the Kansas City Athletics, and the Minnesota Twins. Time and time again, he awed crowds and players alike with his dramatic catches. And while Bill Tuttle will long be remembered for his ability to play the game, his legacy goes way beyond the baseball diamond.

A Dangerous Habit Begins

William Tuttle was born on July 4, 1929, in Farmington, Illinois. He played baseball in college before joining the Detroit Tigers minor-league system. He bounced around the minor leagues before finally making it to the majors. It was there that Tuttle followed in the footsteps of so many "boys of summer" and picked up the habit of chewing tobacco.

According to Tuttle, after an injury sidelined him, he quickly grew bored sitting on the bench. Teammate Harvey Kuenn offered him a chew to pass the time. Those first days of chewing on the bench became years of tobacco use on and off the field. Tuttle chewed for almost forty years, sometimes ten to twelve hours a day. Many of the outfielder's baseball cards show the young player with a cheek bulging with chewing tobacco.

Illness Strikes

Thirty-eight years after it began, Tuttle realized the grave consequences of his habit. In 1993, he was diagnosed with *buccal cancer* that required immediate surgery. The surgery that was supposed to take two or three hours to remove "a little piece" out of his mouth, ended up being much more extensive and took more than thirteen hours. In 1996, Tuttle told *USA Today*: "That little piece turned into the biggest tumor the doctor said he ever took out of someone's mouth."

Tuttle needed even more surgery and cancer treatment. After more than five operations and fifty hours of surgery, Tuttle had lost most of his face, including his jaw, teeth, and right cheek. Tuttle was so disfigured that some of his grandchildren were afraid to see him. What's more, Tuttle and his wife, Gloria, did not have health insurance and could not afford to pay the ever-growing medical bills.

A Fair Trade

Baseball during Tuttle's day was not like baseball today. Players did not make tons of money, and they didn't get

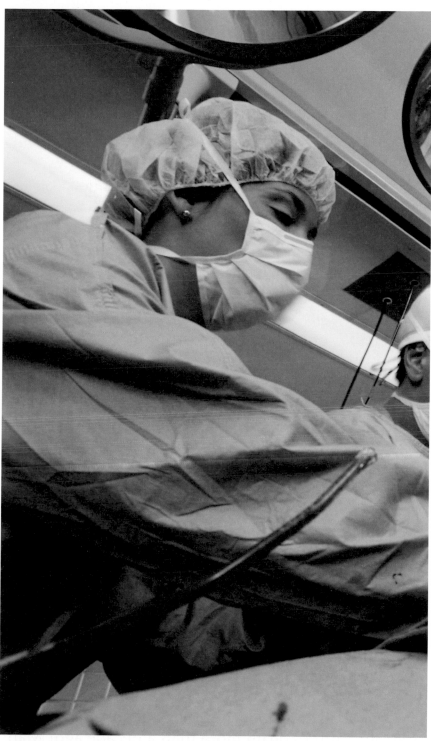

Using smokeless tobacco can have dangerous health effects that may require extensive and life-threatening surgery.

paid to do commercials for products from cereal to shoes to underwear. So Bill Tuttle did not have a lot of money. Luckily, Joe Garagiola, another former baseball player and an announcer, offered to help. As head of the Baseball Assistance Team (BAT), which helps former players, Garagiola called Tuttle and told him BAT would pay his medical bills. But Garagiola wanted Tuttle do something in return.

Garagiola was also head of the National Spit Tobacco Education Program (NSTEP), whose goal is to raise awareness about the dangers of smokeless tobacco. One of NSTEP's targets was major league baseball, because almost 40 percent of the players were using smokeless tobacco. Garagiola asked the Tuttles to help NSTEP achieve its goal.

Although Bill Tuttle was nearing the end of his life, he and his wife agreed to help. Joe and Bill visited several major league baseball teams that spring. According to Garagiola, the players were not receptive at first. Some continued to chew even as Garagiola spoke to them about the dangers. But when he introduced Tuttle, everything changed.

The former baseball player's face told the story: if you continue to chew, you will end up looking like me. He also urged players to remember that they are role models to young people. In some cases, as Tuttle spoke, players took the tobacco from their mouths.

In 1995, Bill Tuttle received the U.S. Surgeon General's highest award, the Exemplary Service Medallion, for his work. Tuttle lost his battle with cancer in 1998, at age sixty-nine.

A Long History

Has baseball's relationship with smokeless tobacco since Bill Tuttle's death more than a decade ago? Many

Many baseball stars continue to use smokeless tobacco.

Chewing tobacco was advertised as a safe alternative to cigarettes. Tobacco companies encouraged this stereotype by offering incentives to use smokeless tobacco.

players say chewing is just part of the game, and the truth is, it has been for a long, long time.

Baseball's Beginnings

Smokeless tobacco was popular in the United States in 1845, which is when people were just learning about the game of baseball. The habit was especially popular among those first players. Back then, the stuff actually served a useful purpose; players used it to keep their mouths moist in dusty ballparks, and then used the saliva to soften their baseball gloves.

According to one study, each day over 2,200 adolescents try smokeless tobacco for the first time and approximately 830 young people become regular users.

(*Source:* American Lung Association)

In the early 1900s, chewing tobacco fell out of favor among the general public—mainly because of the TB scare. But this didn't seem to concern baseball players, who kept on dipping. In fact, the habit may have actually grown among baseball players around this time. That's because this is when the "spitball" became a popular weapon among pitchers. A spitball is a pitch that is delivered with a dab of saliva on the ball. The saliva, it seems, allows the pitcher to put more spin on the ball, making it more difficult to hit. The spitball was banned from baseball in 1920 (though it doesn't mean it doesn't get thrown even today); smokeless tobacco, however, was not.

Smokeless Tobacco Endures

Baseball players continued to use smokeless tobacco through the 1940s, but by the 1950s, the boys of summer started to make the switch to cigarettes. Many were paid to appear in cigarette advertisements.

In 1987, a study showed that almost 35 percent of professional baseball players used chewing tobacco.

But chewing tobacco was never completely gone from baseball. It staged a comeback in the 1970s, primarily because the health effects of smoking were making headlines. To counteract the negative press, tobacco companies touted chewing tobacco and snuff as safe alternatives to cigarettes and as methods to help people kick the smoking habit.

Fortunately, today fewer and fewer baseball players use smokeless tobacco.

To encourage baseball players to use their products, tobacco companies gave free samples to college and professional teams. Their plan worked. By 1985, 40 percent of college baseball players were using smokeless tobacco.

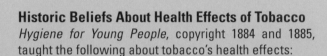

Historic Beliefs About Health Effects of Tobacco
Hygiene for Young People, copyright 1884 and 1885, taught the following about tobacco's health effects:

Sores on the lips, and even cancers, sometimes result from the use of tobacco; the breath, foul and repulsive, shows the condition of the stomach, the tissues, and the blood; the gums of smokers and chewers often become spongy, and their teeth are soiled and dark, instead of being white and pure.

The effect of the poison is to make the mouth dry, thus causing an extra amount of saliva to be poured out from the glands. But the constant spitting of the tobacco juice, robs one of the saliva needed for digestion, and brings on dyspepsia.

Besides doing this harm to the user, the habit of spitting is a very impolite one. It makes floors and sidewalks unfit for cleanly people to walk on, and endangers the clothing of all who are near.

Regarding whether tobacco is a gateway drug, here's what *Hygiene for Young People* indicates was thought in the late 1880s:

In many cases, tobacco acts as the usher at the door of the saloon, because the dryness of the mouth which it produces, makes the user thirsty. But it is not a natural thirst, it can not be satisfied by water; for tobacco so affects the nerves, as often to make one crave another narcotic.

Those in charge of inebriate asylums say that nearly all their patients have been users of tobacco as well as of alcohol.

In 1987, a survey of nearly 300 professional baseball players found that half had a history of using smokeless tobacco; nearly 35 percent were current users.

Baseball Today

Today, many baseball players seem to be getting the message that smokeless tobacco is a deadly habit. A ten-year study concluded in 2006, found that the prevalence of smokeless-tobacco use among players declined from 41 percent at the beginning of the study to 25 percent

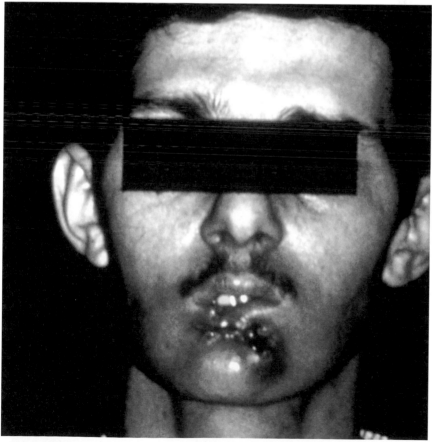

Smokeless tobacco can lead to cancer of the gums, jaw, and lip. This can be especially true in the case of plugs of tobacco, which are held in the front of the mouth between the gums and the lips.

at its conclusion. In addition, players who were using smokeless tobacco at the beginning of the study were likely to have leukoplakia, but as smokeless-tobacco use declined, the presence of the condition also decreased. Researchers also found that many players who used smokeless tobacco wanted to quit, with the percentage of players wanting to quit almost doubling over the course of the study.

Why the positive changes? Researchers believe there are a couple reasons. For one, in 1993, major league baseball banned the use of smokeless tobacco among minor league players, coaches, and umpires. The ban applies to practices, games, and team travel. The National College Athletic Association (NCAA) has a similar ban for college players. The other reason for the smokeless-tobacco decline, researchers believe, is because players are being educated about the ill effects of smokeless tobacco and receive support in their efforts to kick the habit.

Since the minor league ban seems to have been successful in helping players quit smokeless tobacco, why hasn't smokeless tobacco also been banned at the major league level? The main reason is that these players belong to a union that protects the rights of its members. As a result, major league baseball cannot tell the players whether they can use smokeless tobacco. In fact, even major league players who are sent to the minors, after an injury for example, are not held to the minor league smokeless-tobacco ban.

Meanwhile, people like Joe Garagiola would be happy to see a smokeless-tobacco ban put in place for major league baseball—but he knows it may never happen. So instead, Garagiola concentrates his efforts on education and support for those who want to quit. Many people believe that the cycle of tobacco addiction could be stopped if more laws were in place to regulate tobacco and to control how tobacco companies advertise their products.

CHAPTER

Glossary

attorneys general: The chief law officers of states or countries.

entice: To persuade someone do something by offering something desirable in return.

Advertising Smokeless Tobacco

Ads for smokeless tobacco hang at gas stations, baseball parks, and rodeo arenas. They cover the pages of many magazines, too. Advertising, after all, is one of the main things companies do to stay in business. If companies didn't advertise, the general public would not know about their products; if people are not aware of a product, chances are pretty good they won't buy it.

Advertising is not the only way tobacco companies try to *entice* customers, however. Some offer their merchandise at discount prices. Some provide free "gifts," such as T-shirts, key chains, and beach towels, with the purchase of their product.

Others give consumers free samples of their latest and greatest products. And still others try to increase sales by developing new and different products such candy-flavored snuff. Attracting customers in these ways is called marketing.

Most people don't dispute a tobacco company's right to advertise or market its smokeless-tobacco products—to adults. After all, adults are the only people legally allowed to use chewing tobacco and snuff. But many individuals and groups believe tobacco companies do not restrict their advertising and marketing efforts to the adult population. Critics claim tobacco companies target children and teenagers by developing candy-flavored products, using cartoon characters in their advertising, and packaging their products to look like candy. Manufacturers do this, say their opponents, in an effort to lure children into tobacco addiction. After all, a teenager addicted to smokeless tobacco is likely to become a lifelong customer.

The U.S. government has passed legislation to regulate tobacco advertising. Today laws limit where and how tobacco companies are allowed to advertise. Much of this has been done in an effort to shield children and teenagers from taking their first "dip" and hence becoming addicted.

The Smokeless Tobacco Master Settlement Agreement

In 1998, forty-six states joined together to file a lawsuit against the four largest cigarette manufacturers in the United States. The suit was settled when these tobacco companies signed the Master Settlement Agreement (MSA). Four states were not part of the suit because they had settled with the tobacco companies on their own. Among other things, the MSA called for doing away with billboards to advertise tobacco products, use of cartoon characters such as Joe Camel in tobacco

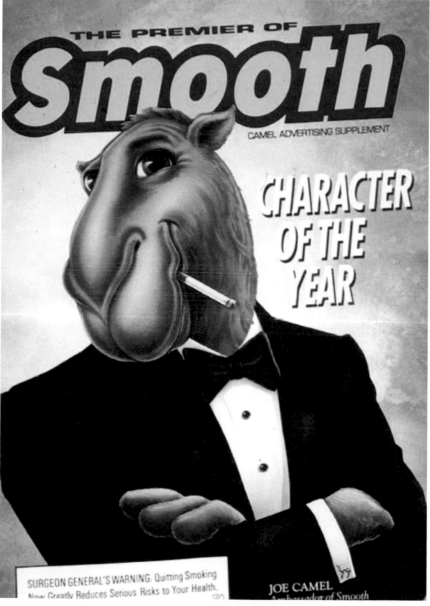

Many people claim that advertisements like this, which used cartoon characters, made smoking more appealing to young people.

advertisements, and marketing tobacco products to youth.

That same year, the *attorneys general* of forty-four states and the U.S. Smokeless Tobacco Company (USSTC), the country's largest smokeless-tobacco manufacturer, signed a similar agreement, called the Smokeless Tobacco Master Settlement Agreement (STMSA). USSTC was the only smokeless-tobacco company to sign the agreement, although there are others who sell the product.

According to the USSTC's Web site, the settlement created a partnership between the company and the participating states that accomplished the following:

- Provided up to $100 million to the American Legacy Foundation over a ten-year period. This foundation uses the money to conduct public-education campaigns and other programs to reduce tobacco use and other substance abuse among children and youth.
- Put restrictions on smokeless-tobacco advertising, including the following:
  — No direct or indirect targeting of youth (persons under age eighteen)
  — No outdoor brand-name advertising (except retail signage under fourteen square feet)
  — No signs in arenas, stadiums, shopping malls, and video arcades
  — No transit advertising (no advertising on buses or trains or at their stops)
- Put restrictions on the way smokeless tobacco is promoted. For example, smokeless-tobacco products cannot be promoted at concerts; events at which children and teenagers are a major part of the audience; events at which paid participants or

contestants are youths; and football, baseball, soccer, basketball, and hockey games.
- Banned the distribution of non-tobacco merchandise displaying the brand name, logo, or trademark of a tobacco product to the general public.
- Limited the distribution of free samples of tobacco products to adult-only facilities or in connection with tobacco purchases at retail locations.

Naturally, since the agreement was signed, people have wanted to know if it has been effective. Is the USSTC holding up its end of the bargain? Are fewer children and teenagers picking up the smokeless-tobacco habit?

The Tobacco Company's View

The U.S. Smokeless Tobacco Company claims it is dedicated to the goals of the STMSA and feels strongly about protecting teenagers from smokeless-tobacco advertising and marketing. The company says its products are for adults only and denies marketing them to teens.

Many organizations have put a lot of effort into stopping children and teenagers from starting to use smokeless tobacco.

The STMSA was a collection of laws made in an attempt to keep children and young adults from starting to use smokeless tobacco.

To prove its efforts are working, the company's Web site cites two national studies that show a drop over the past ten years in the number of teens using smokeless-tobacco products. The two studies are the Monitoring the Future Study (MFS) and the Youth Risk Behavior Surveillance Survey (YRBSS). The company says these are the only national surveys that use consistent methods for reporting data from year to year.

Both surveys show a decrease in underage use of smokeless tobacco among males and females between 1995 and 2006. For example, the MFS shows a 48 percent decrease in current smokeless-tobacco use among eighth-graders, a 40 percent decrease among tenth-graders, and a 50 percent decrease among twelfth-graders. The YRBSS shows a 30 percent decrease among high-school-aged respondents.

The Opposing View

Groups such as the Campaign for Tobacco-Free Kids and the American Lung Association disagree. They feel the USSTC and other tobacco companies recognize the need to get kids hooked on tobacco so they will become lifelong customers. They believe tobacco companies continue to target children through marketing and advertising and are not following the guidelines outlined in the STMSA.

According to the Campaign for Tobacco-Free Kids, one way smokeless-tobacco companies appeal to children is by adding sweet fruit flavorings to their products. The first such product, introduced in 1993 by the USSTC, was a cherry-flavored moist snuff. A former company spokesperson reportedly said the product was "for somebody who likes the taste of candy, if you know what I'm saying." Although the product came out prior to the STMSA, it is still available, along with other flavors such as apple, citrus, peach, vanilla, and berry. According to the company's 2005 Annual Report, flavored products make up more than 11 percent of all moist-snuff sales.

The Campaign for Tobacco-Free Kids also believes that smokeless-tobacco products are still being mar-

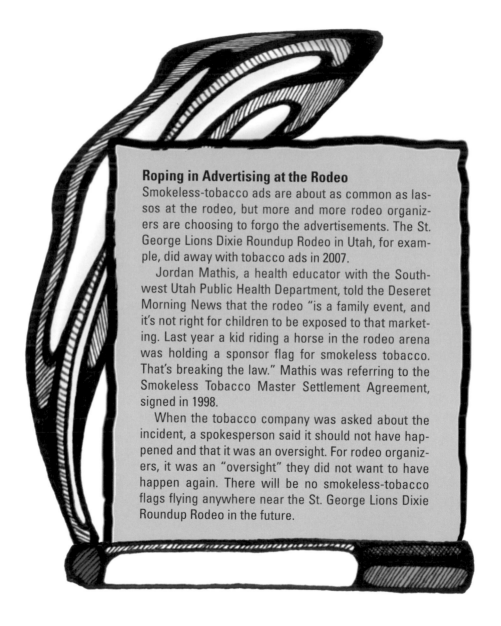

Roping in Advertising at the Rodeo

Smokeless-tobacco ads are about as common as lassos at the rodeo, but more and more rodeo organizers are choosing to forgo the advertisements. The St. George Lions Dixie Roundup Rodeo in Utah, for example, did away with tobacco ads in 2007.

Jordan Mathis, a health educator with the Southwest Utah Public Health Department, told the Deseret Morning News that the rodeo "is a family event, and it's not right for children to be exposed to that marketing. Last year a kid riding a horse in the rodeo arena was holding a sponsor flag for smokeless tobacco. That's breaking the law." Mathis was referring to the Smokeless Tobacco Master Settlement Agreement, signed in 1998.

When the tobacco company was asked about the incident, a spokesperson said it should not have happened and that it was an oversight. For rodeo organizers, it was an "oversight" they did not want to have happen again. There will be no smokeless-tobacco flags flying anywhere near the St. George Lions Dixie Roundup Rodeo in the future.

keted to kids. They say even after the STMSA, smoke-less-tobacco companies continue to sponsor sporting events and teams. For example, the USSTC is a sponsor of both professional motor sports and rodeo bull riding. In addition, tobacco opponents say, the USSTC continues to advertise heavily in magazines that target youth. In 2001, for example, the company spent $9.4 million on such advertising, a 161 percent increase from 1997.

Other Research

A group of researchers wanted to see if the STMSA had been effective in reducing teenagers' exposure to smokeless-tobacco advertising. To do so, they collected data about magazines popular among youth between the ages of twelve and seventeen over a ten-year period. They chose such magazines as *Sports Illustrated*, *Rolling Stone*, *Spin*, and *Sporting News*, then looked to see what kind of advertising appeared in those magazines and who read them.

Results of the study were not very encouraging. At the beginning of the study, 66 percent of young readers were exposed to smokeless-tobacco advertising in these magazines. At the end of the study, 64 percent were exposed to such ads. What do those numbers mean? They mean nothing changed over the course of ten years. At either end of the study, about two-thirds of America's youth were exposed to smokeless-tobacco advertising in magazines. What's more, the researchers found that smoke-less-tobacco advertising in magazines actually increased in the first year after the STMSA went into effect, reaching 83 percent of teenagers. In 2000, that number dropped to 57 percent, but each year after that, the number rose steadily again, reaching 64 percent in 2002.

Tobacco advertisements now must conform to harsh regulations; where and how tobacco products can be advertised is controlled by the MSA.

Federal Regulation?

For years Congress has been considering further legislation that would curb some of the tobacco industry's most common marketing tactics—including multi-container discounts, gifts with purchase, and lower prices. If the law passes, the Food and Drug Administration (FDA) will have authority over tobacco products, including the right to regulate any marketing that targets children. The FDA is part of the U.S. government and oversees

Opposition to Tobacco Use
Throughout history there have been people and governments opposed to tobacco. Here are some examples:

- Tobacco was illegal in Japan in 1590. If caught using tobacco, users lost their property or were sent to jail.
- In the early 1600s, King James VI of Scotland increased taxes on tobacco by 4,000 percent! He did this because he was strongly against smoking. King James hoped imposing such a tax would discourage people from bringing the plant into the country.
- A Chinese law in 1683 threatened to behead anyone found in possession of tobacco.
- Russian czar Michael Fedorovich, who was in power from 1613 to 1645, forbade the sale of tobacco, declaring users would be physically punished and persistent users would be killed.

The Campaign for Tobacco-Free Kids has been trying to get Congress to pass a law that would allow the FDA to regulate tobacco products, especially in regards to how they are sold and advertised to children.

the safety of most drugs and foods sold in the country. To many, it is pretty surprising that the FDA does not already regulate tobacco. In 2004, Congress came close to passing this legislation, but not close enough. The Campaign for Tobacco-Free Kids, along with many other groups and organizations, has been urging Congress to pass the law as soon as possible. In fact, a recent national poll found that 70 percent of voters support Congress passing the legislation.

If and when the law passes to give the FDA authority to regulate tobacco products, the FDA would be able to do the following:

- restrict tobacco advertising and promotions, especially to children
- stop illegal sales of tobacco products to children
- completely ban candy-flavored cigarettes, which many believe are starter products for young, new smokers
- require changes in tobacco products, such as the removal of harmful ingredients and the reduction of nicotine levels
- prohibit health claims about tobacco products that are not scientifically proven to work, discourage current smokers from quitting, or encourage nonsmokers to start
- require tobacco companies to reveal the contents of, changes to, and research about the health effects of their products
- require larger and more informative health warnings on tobacco products
- prohibit use of terms such as "light," "mild," and "low-tar," which mislead consumers into believing that certain cigarettes are safer than others.

The smoker's guide to low-tar cigarettes.

With all the controversy about smoking going on, lots of smokers are deciding to switch to low-tar cigarettes.

But which low-tar cigarette should a switcher switch to?

Well, here's an easy guide to follow.

First, there are those so-called new cigarettes claiming scientific breakthrough and hyped-up flavor. Unfortunately there's nothing very revolutionary about the way they taste.

Next there are those brands that promise nothing but low-tar numbers. They're fine if low numbers are all you want. Because their scientific filters work so well, they filter out most of the taste.

Fortunately there is an alternative. Vantage. The low-tar cigarette that's different from all the others.

From the very beginning Vantage was designed to deliver flavor like a full-flavor cigarette with less tar than 95% of all cigarettes. So forget all those empty promises and go with the real flavor of Vantage.

It will probably turn out to be the only low-tar cigarette you'll enjoy.

Regular, Menthol, and new Vantage 100's.

Warning- The Surgeon General Has Determined That Cigarette Smoking Is Dangerous to Your Health.

FILTER 10 mg "tar", 0.7 mg nicotine, MENTHOL 11 mg "tar", 0.7 mg nicotine, av. per cigarette, FTC Report DEC '78; FILTER 100's, 11 mg "tar", 0.8 mg nicotine av. per cigarette, by FTC method.

Historically, tobacco ads have touted low tar cigarettes as healthier alternatives to regular tobacco products. However, the truth is that these can be just as harmful.

Advertisements may make tobacco products look enticing, but the best advice is to never take that first puff or chew. Whether it's cigarettes, cigars, chewing tobacco, or snuff, kicking the tobacco habit is tough for anyone who has become a user, regardless of that person's age. Once nicotine grabs hold, even the strongest-willed person will find quitting difficult.

CHAPTER 6

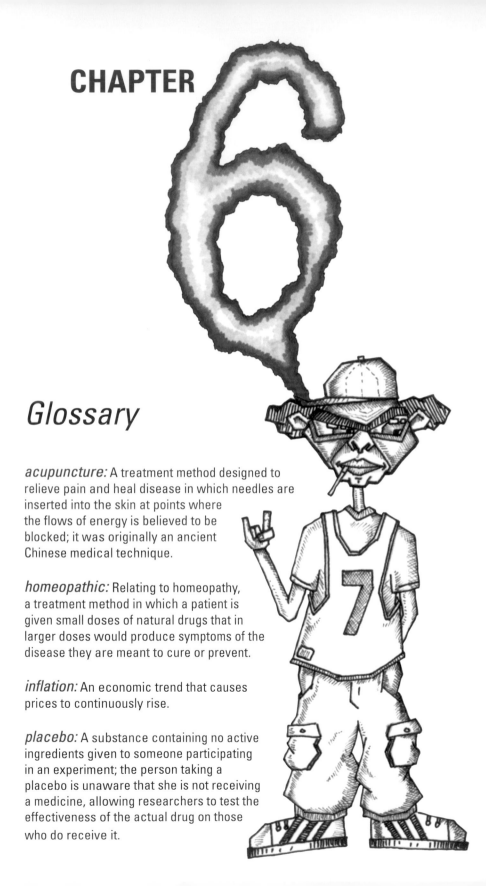

Glossary

acupuncture: A treatment method designed to relieve pain and heal disease in which needles are inserted into the skin at points where the flows of energy is believed to be blocked; it was originally an ancient Chinese medical technique.

homeopathic: Relating to homeopathy, a treatment method in which a patient is given small doses of natural drugs that in larger doses would produce symptoms of the disease they are meant to cure or prevent.

inflation: An economic trend that causes prices to continuously rise.

placebo: A substance containing no active ingredients given to someone participating in an experiment; the person taking a placebo is unaware that she is not receiving a medicine, allowing researchers to test the effectiveness of the actual drug on those who do receive it.

Time to Quit

The long list of health problems caused by smokeless tobacco should be enough to make anyone want to quit—or never start in the first place. After all, who wants to lose his teeth and have mouth sores and painful gums? Who wants to lose half her face to cancer? Who wants to end up paralyzed—or worse, dead—because of a heart attack or stroke? Nobody does.

But many people who chew or dip believe they will never pay the consequences. They believe those horrible things happen only to other people. *Dreadful health consequences don't happen to young people; there's plenty of time to quit,* they may think. *Quitting is no big deal; it's not as hard as people say it is.* Unfortunately, this type of wishful thinking, denial, and fantasy cannot fight cancer or heart disease.

In addition to avoiding the health effects of smokeless tobacco, there are other reasons to quit. For one, the habit is expensive, and the more a person uses, the more expensive it gets. Inflation pretty much ensures the cost of tobacco will continue to rise. Second, using tobacco products is becoming less and less socially acceptable. Few people want to be around someone who has brown-stained teeth, bad breath, and a mouth filled with gum disease—not to mention the spitting. Finally, using tobacco sets a bad example for others—especially children. Even teenagers need to realize that they are role models for the youngsters around them.

It's Hard to Quit

Nicotine addiction is why quitting any tobacco product is difficult. Nicotine does not stay in the body for very long, and as soon as nicotine levels diminish in the blood, the body starts to react. According to the American Cancer Society, when a person addicted to nicotine tries to quit by stopping abruptly, she almost immediately experiences the following symptoms:

- dizziness
- depression
- frustration
- anger
- irritability
- trouble sleeping
- trouble concentrating
- restlessness
- headaches
- tiredness
- fatigue
- increased appetite

Nicotine withdrawal can lead to uncomfortable symptoms, including headaches and irritability. This is because the body feels like it needs nicotine to function; it is physicaly dependant on the drug.

Not everyone experiences all these symptoms, and symptoms diminish as time passes. Unfortunately, taking a dip or chew will almost immediately alleviate these unpleasant symptoms. That's why people trying to quit are so quick to jump right back into the habit.

Quitting Smokeless Tobacco Is Different

While quitting a nicotine habit is difficult for anyone, smokeless-tobacco users tend to face an extra challenge. Because dippers and chewers are so used to having something inside their mouths, they often have a stronger need than smokers for something to take the place of tobacco.

On the other hand, those who use smokeless tobacco tend to see the benefits of quitting sooner than smokers do. That's because mouth sores and gum problems caused by chewing tobacco and snuff usually begin to heal quickly. For some, this outweighs the withdrawal symptoms and can help motivate them to quit for good.

How to Quit

No two smokeless-tobacco users are alike. Each user started using the smokeless tobacco for a different reason, and each has to come to his or her own decision to quit. Oftentimes people who are forced to quit have little success; a person needs to be self-motivated in order to stop using smokeless tobacco for good. Each person who makes the decision to quit will find success in his or her own individual way, but can help to know what has worked for others.

People can choose from several quitting methods. Some quitters will be successful on their first attempt, while others will need to try and try again. They can join support groups. They may use a nicotine replacement (described later in this chapter). They might decide to quit suddenly, or go "cold turkey." They may try the same method over and over again, or use a different one each time they make the commitment to quit. Ultimately, it does not matter what method a person uses—as long as it works.

> **Just Another Form of Smokeless Tobacco**
>
> As more and more public places go smoke free, tobacco companies are offering new products for smokers. Lozenges fused with tobacco and small tobacco-containing pouches are being sold as alternative ways to get that nicotine fix. While some companies may advertise these products as quitting aids, they are just different forms of smokeless tobacco that allow smokers, dippers, and chewers more opportunities to indulge in the tobacco habit.

Getting Support

Some people trying to quit smokeless tobacco want support from others. Most states offer some type of telephone-based quitting program. A person trying to quit can talk to a trained professional, who can offer support, information, and advice. Professional support can also be found at hospitals, schools, and many workplaces. Doctors, nurses, and counselors can refer a person who wants to quit to the appropriate place for help.

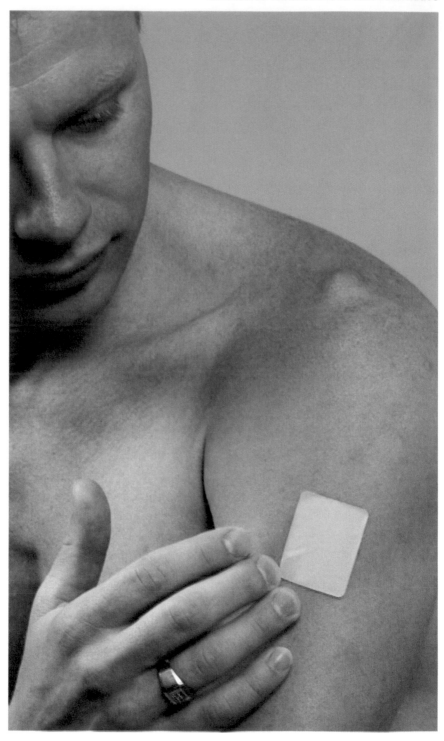

Nicotine patches can help people quit cigarettes, but they have not yet been definitively shown to help people who are addicted to smokeless tobacco.

Studies have found that the best support programs include either individual or group counseling. People who receive professional counseling tend to be more successful at quitting. And the more intense the counseling—the greater the duration and frequency of the sessions—the more successful a person will usually be.

Quitting with Medication?

Because nicotine causes such intense withdrawal symptoms, people who want to quit smoking often find success with nicotine replacement therapy (NRT). These medications deliver nicotine to the body without the other components of tobacco smoke. When used with counseling, NRT has proven successful at helping many people kick their tobacco habits.

The FDA has approved several NRTs for smokers; each delivers nicotine to the body in a different way. NRTs are available in the following forms:

- gum
- patches
- lozenges
- inhalers
- nasal sprays

Though these therapies have been successful for smokers, they have not been approved specifically for people wanting to quit smokeless tobacco. That's because there is not yet enough scientific evidence that they work for this population. More and larger studies need to be done. So far, NRTs seem to help a person feel better in the first few weeks after ending smokeless-tobacco use, but they do not yet appear to help in the long term.

While not specifically approved to help smokeless-tobacco users quit, some types of nicotine replacement may be more helpful for this purpose than others. These include nicotine gum and lozenges, simply because they help keep the mouth busy. This seems to make them a good substitute for smokeless tobacco.

Other Medications on the Horizon

NRTs are not the only medications available to help people kick the nicotine habit. Buproprion, a prescription drug, helps reduce withdrawal symptoms in smokers by affecting the chemicals in the brain related to nicotine cravings. So far, it is not clear whether buproprion is as effective for smokeless-tobacco users as it is for smokers. A study in 2007 found the medication helped reduce cravings in people who were trying to quit smokeless tobacco. However, the group taking bupropion was no more successful at quitting than the group taking a *placebo*.

Varenicline, another prescription medication used for nicotine addiction, may be more effective than buproprion at lessening withdrawal symptoms. Again, however, medical studies are needed to see if it is an effective aid for quitting smokeless tobacco.

New Products to Help Quitters

Several other products are available that may or may not be effective at helping smokeless-tobacco users quit. They are not drugs, so the FDA does not regulate them, and they should not be used without first consulting a doctor or other health-care professional.

Non-tobacco snuff is one such product. Like moist snuff, it comes packaged in tins and is available in different flavors. Made from ingredients such as tea, mint leaves, alfalfa, and clover, non-tobacco snuff may be used alone or with tobacco snuff as a way to gradually wean oneself off nicotine. No medical studies have been done to prove whether this product works.

Alternative Therapies

Many smokeless-tobacco users turn to alternative therapies to help them quit. These methods include *acupuncture*, hypnosis, *homeopathic* remedies, herbal supplements, and tobacco deterrents that, supposedly, change the taste of tobacco, thus making it less appealing to use.

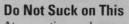

Do Not Suck on This
At one time, pharmacies made nicotine lollipops that contained a substance called nicotine salicylate and sweeteners. Nicotine salicylate is not approved by the FDA for pharmacy use, and the FDA warned pharmacies to stop selling the nicotine suckers, saying, "The candy-like products present a risk of accidental use by children."

Some people swear by each of these methods, but none has been scientifically proven to help people quit the nicotine habit. For any alternative therapy, it is always a good idea to check with a doctor or other health-care professional for advice or a referral before beginning use.

Quitting for Good

When a person makes the decision to quit using smokeless tobacco, the following tips can help lead to success:

- Set a quit date. People who decide to quit should choose a date and mark the date on a calendar. It also helps to tell others of the date.

Medical doctors can give advice about how best to go about quitting, as well as offer information about support networks and prescribe medications to help alleviate withdrawal symptoms.

- Talk to a doctor. Doctors can offer advice and support, and, if necessary, they can prescribe medications.
- Get counseling. Individual or group counseling helps tobacco users quit for good. In group counseling, people meet others who understand what they are going through. Group members support each other and offer advice.
- Use nicotine replacements. Gum and lozenges, especially, can help reduce withdrawal symptoms and fill the need to have something in the mouth.
- Plan ahead, be prepared. People trying to quit need a plan for how to deal with withdrawal symptoms and the subsequent urge to give up. For example, they should have plenty of licorice, chewing gum, hard candy, sunflower seeds, and more on hand. Putting something else in the mouth can help break that tobacco-chewing habit. Individuals can also go for a walk, call a friend, or do some other activity until the cravings subside.

Quitting often takes practice. But as the old saying goes, "If at first you don't succeed, try, try again." After all, the more times you do something, the more likely your are to succeed—and the more a person tries to quit, the more apt he or she will be to eventually succeed.

In the United States, 7.8 million people age twelve and older regularly use smokeless tobacco.

(*Source:* American Lung Association, 2006)

Further Reading

Balkin, Karen (ed.). *Tobacco and Smoking: Opposing Viewpoints.* San Diego, Calif.: Greenhaven Press, 2005.

Bellenir, Karen (ed.). *Tobacco Information for Teens: Health Tips About the Hazards of Using Cigarettes, Smokeless Tobacco, and Other Nicotine Products.* Detroit, Mich.: Omnigraphics, 2007.

Bernards, Neal. *Advertising: Distinguishing Between Fact and Opinion.* San Diego, Calif.: Greenhaven Press, 2005.

Gately, Iain. *Tobacco: A Cultural History of How an Exotic Plant Seduced Civilization.* New York: Grove Press, 2001.

Goodman, Jordan (ed.). *Tobacco in History and Culture: An Encyclopedia.* Farmington Hills, Mich.: Thomson Gale, 2005.

Green, Carl R. *Nicotine and Tobacco.* Berkeley Heights, N.J.: MyReportLinks.com Books, 2005.

Heyes, Eileen. *Tobacco U.S.A.: The Industry Behind the Smoke Curtain.* Minneapolis, Minn.: Twenty-First Century Books, 2001.

For More Information

American Cancer Society
www.cancer.org

Centers for Disease Control and Prevention Office on
Smoking and Health
www.cdc.gov/tobacco/smokeless/index.htm

National Institute of Dental and Craniofacial Research
www.nidcr.nih.gov/HealthInformation/
DiseasesAndConditions/SpitTobacco/default.htm

National Spit Tobacco Education Program (NSTEP)
www.nstep.org

Nemours Foundation
kidshealth.org/teen/drug_alcohol/tobacco/
smokeless.html

Publisher's note:
The Web sites listed on this page were active at the time of publication. The
publisher is not responsible for Web sites that have changed their addresses or
discontinued operation since the date of publication. The publisher will review
and update the Web-site list upon each reprint.

Bibliography

American Cancer Society. "Child and Teen Tobacco Use." www.cancer.org/docroot/PED/content/PED_10_2X_Child_and_Teen_Tobacco_Use.asp?sitearea=PED.

American Cancer Society. "Smokeless Tobacco." www.cancer.org/docroot/PED/content/PED_10_13X_Quitting_Smokeless_Tobacco.asp?sitearea=&level=.

American Lung Association, "Smokeless Tobacco Factsheet." http://www.lungusa.org/site/pp.asp?c=dvLUK9O0E&b=1694879.

Bird, Patrick J. "History of Chewing Tobacco Among Baseball Players." *Keeping Fit.* University of Florida College of Health and Human Performance. www.hhp.ufl.edu/faculty/pbird/keepingfit/ARTICLE/History.htm.

Campaign for Tobacco-Free Kids. "New Poll: Voters Strongly Support FDA Regulation of Tobacco, Say It Would Be Important Accomplishment for Congress" (press release), July 16, 2007. www.tobaccofreekids.org.

Campaign for Tobacco-Free Kids. "Special Report: FDA Authority Over Tobacco," October 4, 2007. tobaccofreekids.org/reports/fda.

Centers for Disease Control and Prevention. "Topics in Minority Health—Prevalence of Oral Lesions and Smokeless Tobacco Use in Northern Plains Indians." *MMWR Weekly*, October 7, 1988. ier.isclii.es/mmwr/preview/mmwrhtml/00001287.htm.

Centers for Disease Control and Prevention, "Smoking and Tobacco Use Fact Sheet," 2007. www.cdc.gov/tobacco/data_statistics/Factsheet/smokeless_tobacco.htm.

Cooper, Jeff, James A. Ellison, and Margaret M. Walsh. "Spit (Smokeless)-Tobacco Use by Baseball Players Entering the Professional Ranks." *Journal of Athletic Training* 28 (June 2003).

Fahmy, Sam. "UGA Study: Youth Exposed to Smokeless Tobacco Ads Despite Settlement" (press release), University of Georgia, October 4, 2007. www.eurekalert.org/pub_releases/2007-10/uog-usy100407.php.

Hale, J., and J. Blackwell, "Quitting Smokeless Tobacco" (Patient handout). *Evidence-Based Practice* 9(4) (2006).

Imholte, Jane. "Obituary: Anti-Spit Tobacco Crusader Bill Tuttle." *Tobacco Control* 7 (1998): 443–444.

Imholte, Jane. "A Girl and Her Chew: One Woman's Story of Spit Tobacco Use." *Tobacco Control* 8 (1999): 217–218.

Koenig, Bill. "Former Player Preaches Evils of Cancer-Causing Chewing Tobacco." *USA Today Baseball Weekly*, June 6, 1996. www.usatoday.com/sports/baseball/sbbw0429.htm.

Lee, Jason W., and Gayle Bush. "Tobacco Sponsorship in Sport: Sending the Wrong Message." *Outside the Box,* January 25, 2005. spectrum.troy.edu/~aisfm/tobacco.htm

LeMaster, P. L., C. M. Connell, C. M. Mitchell, and S. M. Manson. "Tobacco Use Among American Indian Adolescents: Protective and Risk Factors." www.ncbi.nlm.nih.gov/sites/entrez?cmd=Retrieve&db=PubMed&dopt=AbstractPlus&list_uids=12039512.

Lester, Greg. "Smokeless Tobacco More Effective than Cigarettes for Delivering Dangerous Carcinogens in the Body, Researchers Say." American Association for Cancer Research, August 9, 2007. www.aacr.org/home/about-us/news.aspx?d=808.

MayoClinic.com. "Chewing Tobacco: Not a Risk-Free Alternative to Cigarettes," October 25, 2005. www.mayoclinic.com/print/chewing-tobacco/CA00019/METHOD.

Medical News Today. "Smokeless Tobacco Use Declining Among Professional Baseball Players—Study Links Steady Decline in Use and Prevalence of Oral Lesions," July 11, 2006. www.medicalnewstoday.com.

National Cancer Institute. "Smokeless Tobacco and Cancer: Questions and Answers," May 30, 2003. www.cancer.gov/cancertopics/factsheet/Tobacco/smokeless.

Nelson, David E., Paul Mowery, Scott Tomar, Stephen Marcus, Gary Giovino, and Luhua Zhao. "Trends in Smokeless Tobacco Use Among Adults and Adolescents." *American Journal of Public Health* 96 (5): 897–905.

Oral Cancer Foundation. "Sean Marsee." www.oralcancerfoundation.org/people/sean_marsee.htm.

Pathfinder Series, No. 2. *Hygiene for Young People.* New York and Chicago: A. S. Barnes and Company, 1884 and 1885.

Perkins, Nancy. "Rodeo Officials Rail Against Tobacco Ads." *Deseret Morning News,* September 6, 2007. desertenews.com/article/content/mobile/0,5223,695207550,00.html.

"Smokeless Tobacco Use in Alaska." *State of Alaska Epidemiology Bulletin.* 8 (4). www.epi.alaska.gov/bulletins/docs/rr2004_04.pdf.

U.S. Centers for Disease Control and Prevention. "Fact Sheet: Betel Quid with Tobacco (Gutka)," February 2007. www.cdc.gov/tobacco/data_statistics/Factsheets/betel_quid.htm.

U.S. Centers for Disease Control and Prevention. "Fact Sheet: Smokeless Tobacco," April 2007. www.cdc.gov/tobacco/data_statistics/Factsheets/smokeless_tobacco.html.

Ziad, Arabi. "An Epidemic that Deserves More Attention: Epidemiology, Prevention, and Treatment of Smokeless Tobacco." *Southern Medical Journal* 100 (9): 890–894.

Index

Picture Credits

Corbis: pp. 42, 98

Creative Commons
Attribution-Share Alike 2.0
Generic
   Guano: p. 67

Dreamstime
   Bobbinholmes: p. 14
   Ckalt: p. 86
   Cmcderm1: p. 71
   Costa007: p. 31
   DJaperman: p. 54
   Daniel 76: p. 70
   Lenm: p. 88

istockphoto.com
   ChristianAnthony: p. 34
   Cjmckendry: p. 23
   Laskowski, Marcin p. 33
   Nicholas, Greg: p. 39
   Obukhov, Dmitry p. 102

Jupiter Images: pp. 13, 95

Office of Applied Statistics:
p. 82

National Cancer Institute:
pp. 46, 73

National Science Foundation
   Deretsky,Zina p. 50

TobaccoDocuments.org: p.
68
   RJ Reynolds Tobacco Co.:
p. 79, 90

U.S. Army Medical
Department Activity –
Alaska: p. 49

United States Army Center
for Health Promotion
and Preventive Medicine
(USACHPPM): pp. 17

To the best knowledge of the publisher, all other images are in the public domain. If any image has been inadvertently uncredited, please notify Harding House Publishing Service, Vestal, New York 13850, so that rectification can be made for future printings.

Author/Consultant Biographies

Author

Katie John Sharp writes fiction and nonfiction books from her home in St. Louis, Missouri. Growing up with a father who smoked unfiltered cigarettes, she witnessed firsthand what tobacco can do to a person and his family. With two teenagers of her own, she knows children need accurate information about cigarettes and other drugs. That's one reason she has written several books and articles about health- and medical-related topics for children.

Consultant

Wade Berrettini, the consultant for *Smoking: The Dangerous Addiction*, received his MD from Jefferson Medical College and a PhD in Pharmacology from Thomas Jefferson University. For ten years, Dr. Berrettini served as a Fellow at the National Institutes of Health in Bethesda, Maryland, where he studied the genetics of behavioral disorders. Currently Dr. Berrettini is the Karl E. Rickels Professor of Psychiatry and Director, Center for Neurobiology and Behavior at the University of Pennsylvania in Philadelphia. He is also an attending physician at the Hospital of the University of Pennsylvania.

Dr. Berrettini is the author or co-author of more than 250 scientific articles as well as several books. He has conducted ground-breaking genetic research in nicotine addiction. He is the holder of two patents and the recipient of several awards, including recognition by Best Doctors in America 2003–2004, 2005–2006, and 2007–2008.